HOMECOOKED

HOMECOOKED

FAVOURITE RECIPES FROM AUSTRALIAN KITCHENS

RECIPES SELECTED BY MAGGIE BEER,
VALLI LITTLE AND IAN MCNAMARA

ABC
Books

Published by ABC Books for the
AUSTRALIAN BROADCASTING CORPORATION
GPO Box 9994 Sydney NSW 2001

Copyright © in this collection Australian Broadcasting Corporation 2006
Copyright © in individual recipes resides with the contributors

First published in April 2006

ISBN 0 7333 1587 9.

Cover and internal design by Christabella Designs
Typeset in 10 on 13.5pt Sabon by Kirby Jones
Printed and bound in Australia by Ligare, Sydney

2 4 5 3 1

Contents

INTRODUCTION

I can tell a good home cook a mile away. They are always warm and welcoming people. In fact I have never met a person who loves cooking that I haven't instantly liked. That is why, when I first read the manuscript for *Homecooked*, I felt that I knew personally all the wonderful people who have kindly donated their tried and trusted recipes.

This is the sort of food I want to cook at home; not the recipes of Michelin-star chefs (I go out to restaurants for those), but from those who learnt as I did, standing at my mother's side at the kitchen stove watching, learning and tasting, and then adapting those recipes over the years to make them their own.

Many of the recipes have been handed down through the generations and often originated in far-off lands, but now, with one quick trip to the supermarket, we can taste the foods of these wonderful places without even leaving home. Whether European, Asian or Australian in its heritage, a home-cooked recipe knows no borders.

To me this book is like an old friend. There is a generosity and honesty about it that comes from the fact that the recipes come from the very heart of the Australian kitchen.

To cook and be cooked for is one of the most precious things we can experience – so enjoy!

Happy cooking,

VALLI

Valli Little
Food Editor
delicious. magazine

LIGHT MEALS

DAVE'S FRENCH CRUMPETS
Serves 1 (multiply as required)

The story behind this recipe is quite simple; I love eggs and I love crumpets. One morning I looked in the fridge and there they both were, and I thought of French Toast and I thought, why not French Crumpet?

INGREDIENTS
2 eggs
sea salt and freshly ground pepper
2 crumpets
butter, to cook
grated cheese and/or cooked bacon, to serve

METHOD
Beat the eggs in a bowl of similar diameter to the crumpet. Season with salt and pepper to taste. Lightly toast the crumpet then soak briefly in egg mixture. Melt the butter in a frying pan. Cook both sides of the crumpet, pouring any extra egg mixture on top while cooking. Serve topped with grated cheese and/or bacon.

Note: To make sweet crumpets, beat 1 egg per 2 crumpets. Add ¼ cup milk, flavour with ¼ teaspoon salt, ½ teaspoon vanilla essence and a pinch of ground nutmeg. Serve sprinkled with ground cinnamon and sugar.

Dave Barham, Nelson Bay, NSW

Eggs 'Malesh'

Serves 2

I started cooking eggs like this after our first trip to the Middle East 15 years ago. We had variations of the egg/lemon/mint/cumin combination, but this is the version that we developed at home. It has become a firm favourite for Sunday brekky. By the way, 'malesh' means 'no worries'.

Spicy grilled sausage and grilled tomato go well with these eggs. Tomatoes can also be dusted with the cumin and mint to serve.

Ingredients

1 tablespoon extra virgin olive oil
4 eggs
1 tablespoon lemon juice
1 teaspoon ground cumin
pinch or two of sea salt
good grind of black pepper
1 tablespoon chopped mint

Method

Heat the oil in a frying pan. Crack the eggs and slide into the hot oil. Immediately sprinkle over the lemon juice, cumin, salt, pepper, and lastly the mint. Cook to your liking, and serve on toast.

Susan Cole, North Perth, WA

BACON AND EGG PIE
Serves 6

I like this recipe because of the nourishing contents, and also because it is easy to prepare ahead and to reheat at breakfast time. These days it is most important to start the day full of energy for school, work or sport. As a collector of well tried recipes, I can recommend this one.

INGREDIENTS
2 sheets frozen shortcrust pastry, thawed
4 bacon rashes, chopped
sliced tomatoes, to layer
½ cup (45g) chopped mushrooms
¼ cup parsley, chopped
5 eggs, beaten
½ cup (125 ml) cream
sea salt and freshly ground pepper
milk to glaze

METHOD
Preheat the oven to 180°C. Line a pie dish with one sheet of pastry, and blind bake until golden.

Arrange layers of bacon, tomatoes, mushrooms and parsley over the pastry. In a bowl beat the eggs and cream gently and season with salt and pepper to taste. Pour mixture over the filling.

Cut the remaining pastry sheet into strips and arrange over the pie in a lattice pattern. Trim and crimp the edges. Glaze the pastry with milk.

Bake for 25–30 minutes, until golden brown.

Ramona Perry, Beachport, SA

PUMPKIN TART
Serves 6–8

This recipe comes from Lorraine in France, but I have adapted it to Oz pumpkin and served it in Sydney for 35 years. Delish!

INGREDIENTS
1⅔ cups (250 g) plain flour
125 g cold butter, chopped
1 egg yolk
1–2 tablespoons iced water
chopped chives, to serve
sour cream, to serve

Filling
½ medium Queensland blue pumpkin
5 large eggs
600 ml cream

METHOD
Place the flour and butter into a food processor. Pulse in short bursts until the mixture resembles breadcrumbs. Add the egg yolk and water and pulse until the mixture just comes together. Gently shape the dough into a disc and roll out on a sheet of non-stick baking paper. Grease a 25 cm flan tin with a removable base and line with the pastry. Prick lightly with a fork, and, while you prepare the filling, freeze to avoid shrinkage.

Preheat the oven to 200°C.

To make the filling, peel, chop, and cook the pumpkin. Place into a large bowl and mash well. Add the eggs and cream, and season with salt and pepper. Whip with a whisk or electric beaters. Pour into the frozen pastry base. Cook for 35 minutes until set and slightly golden.

Mix chopped chives into some sour cream and serve with the tart. Eat as an entrée or as lunch with a garden salad.

Jeanne Marie Thomas, Surry Hills, NSW

SWEET CORN FRITTERS WITH AVOCADO AND TOMATO SALSA

Serves 6

Fritters are loved by everyone, but sweet corn is at the top of the hit parade. In the Tweed, the growers sell this magic summer food off the back of trucks to the passing parade. Steamed cobs with butter, pepper and salt take some beating, but try this wonderfully light fritter concept. The buttermilk provides a sour contrast to the sweet corn.

INGREDIENTS

1 avocado, diced
1 tomato, diced
3 corn cobs
4 tablespoons buttermilk
3 tablespoons plain flour
sea salt and freshly ground pepper
3 eggs, separated
1 tablespoon grated parmesan cheese
3 tablespoons olive, soy or peanut oil

METHOD

Combine the avocado and tomato. Season with salt and pepper to taste and set aside while you make the fritters. Steam the corn cobs and allow to cool. Using a sharp knife, remove the kernels from the cob. Warm kernels in a saucepan with the buttermilk. Remove from the heat, add the flour and season with sea salt and pepper, mix well. Add the egg yolks and cheese to the mixture and combine. Beat the egg whites until firm peaks form. Using a spatula, fold into the corn mixture.

Heat 2 tablespoons of the oil in a heavy based frying pan over medium heat, and place in some greased egg rings. Spoon 2 heaped tablespoons of the mixture into the egg rings and cook for 2 minutes. Flip over and cook until golden brown. Drain on paper towels, and keep hot in a warm oven while you cook the rest. Add the remaining oil as needed.

To serve place a spoonful of the salsa onto each plate, and serve two fritters per person.

Note: You could use 2 cups (400 g) well-drained corn kernels if you can't get fresh corn on the cob.

Anne Fuller, Terranora, NSW

Pepperoni ripieni
Serves 4

I have a Sicilian recipe that I have been cooking for years, which was handed over to me by my father about 25 years ago. A lovely stuffed capsicum with a sweet and savoury filling, with definite Arab influences. Sicily's history clearly shows a long Arab influence. It is defined as being part of Italy but I love the fact that their food has some delicious influences from the Arabs. I won't go into all of Sicily's fare but you must try this gorgeous stuffed capsicum. The best part is that the filling can be used for meat and also squid!

I now run my father's restaurant, which was established in 1970. He has passed away but I love to teach people how to cook and I run small Italian cooking classes within the restaurant.

Of course, one of the fabulous recipes I teach is this one. Many have embraced it and now it may slowly become Newcastle fare for some. Eat it hot or cold, for lunch or dinner or on a picnic the next day.

Ingredients

5 tablespoons olive oil

50 g pine nuts

2 medium onions, chopped

4 ripe tomatoes, chopped

50 g currants

1 cup (100 g) grated parmesan cheese

1 cup (60 g) fresh breadcrumbs

½ bunch flat leaf parsley, chopped

2 red capsicums

METHOD

Preheat the oven to 180°C. Grease a baking tray with oil.

Heat the olive oil in a pan, and add the pine nuts and onions. Cook over low heat until the pine nuts are golden brown. Add the tomatoes and continue to cook until softened. Season with salt to taste. Set aside to cool then add the currants, parmesan, breadcrumbs and parsley. Mix all the ingredients well.

Cut the capsicums in half lengthwise and remove the seeds and membrane. Spoon the filling into the capsicums. Place onto the prepared baking tray. Cover with foil and bake for about 1¾ hours. Rotate the capsicums occasionally so that they cook evenly.

Remove foil the last 15 minutes for a crispy finish.

Maria Licata, Islington, NSW

SARDINIAN-STYLE ARTICHOKE PIE

Serves 8

This dish was one of many served to my husband and I on our visit to family in Alghero, Sardinia. The family owns a vineyard; the property mainly produces grapes, but also olives and figs. The womenfolk pick the grapes during the week which are stored in a large shed on the property. At weekends, the family gathers for the pressing of the grapes in readiness for the annual wine making. A large pot of soup or stew is cooked on the premises and everyone brings their own special dish for the lunch. We thoroughly enjoyed the day, the camaraderie and the 'getting to know' family members that my husband had not seen for 48 years. Of course, we drank the previous year's wine with our meals.

INGREDIENTS

large knob of butter, melted
1 cup (60 g) fresh white breadcrumbs
1 cup (100 g) freshly grated parmesan cheese
2 x 400 g cans artichoke hearts, drained and sliced
1¼ cups (265 g) black olives, drained and pitted
3 tablespoons small capers, drained
200 g diced Italian tomatoes
sea salt and freshly ground pepper
250 g gruyere (or similar) cheese, thinly sliced

Method

Preheat the oven to 180°C.

Brush the sides and base of a 23 cm round springform tin with a little of the melted butter, then scatter over one quarter of the breadcrumbs. In a bowl, mix the remaining breadcrumbs with the parmesan cheese and set aside.

Next, make two layers of ingredients in the tin in this order: artichoke slices, olives, capers, tomatoes, a sprinkling of salt and a good grind of pepper, cheese slices, then a sprinkling of the breadcrumb mixture. Pat the surface of the pie gently then drizzle the remaining melted butter over the top.

Stand the tin over a large sheet of aluminium foil and fold the edges up around the tin in case it leaks a little.

Bake for approximately 30 minutes, or until bubbling and golden on top. Allow to cool for 10 minutes in the tin. Loosen the foil, undo the springform clip and slide the pie on to a large serving plate. Serve immediately with a tossed green salad.

Greta Piras, Dubbo, NSW

SAVOURY CHEESE TOAST
Serves 4

This is my dad's mother's recipe. Nan didn't really like cooking, unlike my mother's family, but she had some real gems of recipes. This brings back memories of Saturday nights, watching TV. Nan would go out to the kitchen and make this for supper. We didn't have a TV at home, and were subjected to a program which I think was a precursor to Four Corners on the ABC. Savoury Cheese Toast heralded a Dick Francis mystery or something similar. Much looked forward to by my brother and I after the preceding program. How your tastes change with age!

INGREDIENTS
1 cup (125 g) grated cheddar cheese
1 dash Worcestershire sauce
1 dash tomato sauce
cayenne pepper
white pepper
1 bacon rasher, finely chopped
1 egg
4 thick slices bread

METHOD
Preheat the oven to 190°C.

Mix all the ingredients (except the bread) together with a fork, but do not beat. My grandmother buttered the bread, but I don't. Spread the mixture thickly onto the bread, right to the edges. Arrange onto oven trays and bake for about 15 minutes, until bubbly and brown. Cut into fingers to serve. This is delicious with soup in winter.

Carolyn Pearce, Cherrybrook, NSW

NEVER-FAIL CHEESE SOUFFLÉ
Serves 6–8

INGREDIENTS
60 g butter plus extra, to grease
¼ cup (35 g) plain flour
1½ cups (375 ml) milk
1 teaspoon salt
pinch cayenne pepper
2 cups (250 g) grated cheese
6 eggs, separated

METHOD
Preheat the oven to 150°C. Grease a 10-cup capacity ovenproof dish well with butter.

Melt the butter in a saucepan over low heat, add the flour and stir until smooth. Slowly stir in the milk, and cook, stirring constantly, until sauce is smooth and has thickened. Season with salt and cayenne pepper.

Remove from the heat, add the cheese and stir until completely melted and the sauce is smooth. You may need to return it to the heat, stirring constantly until a smooth consistency is achieved.

Beat the egg yolks well in a bowl and pour in a little of the cheese sauce, stirring constantly. Add the egg mixture to the cheese sauce, stirring all the while. Set aside to cool slightly.

Beat the egg whites until stiff. Using a metal spoon, fold them into the cheese mixture a little at a time.

Pour mixture into greased dish. Take a sharp knife and cut right through the mixture about an inch from the side all around the bowl. This forms the cap.

Stand the dish in a larger baking dish half full of water and bake for 1–1¼ hours, until well risen and golden brown on top. Serve immediately.

Lois Benson, Tewantin, QLD

NEPTUNE'S PASTA SAUCE
Serves 4

A quick and easy pasta sauce. It is delicious with all types of pasta, such as tagliatelle or fettuccine. This simple sauce evolved trial by error and has become my husband's favourite pasta sauce. It is foolproof and delicious, quick and timely for Lent.

INGREDIENTS

185 g can tuna in oil
45 g can anchovies, chopped
1–2 garlic cloves, crushed
400 g can diced tomatoes
½ cup (125 ml) tomato purée, or 2 tablespoons tomato paste
    and ¼ cup (60 ml) water
⅓ cup chopped parsley
5–6 basil leaves, chopped (optional)
1 tablespoon capers, drained
freshly ground pepper

METHOD

Empty the can of tuna, including the oil, into a saucepan over medium heat. Add the anchovies (with a little of the oil) and garlic and stir for a minute or two. Add the tomatoes, purée, parsley, basil (if using) and capers. Season with freshly ground black pepper (it should not be necessary to add salt). Reduce the heat when bubbling and cook for about 15–20 minutes. Serve with your favourite pasta.

Greta Piras, Dubbo, NSW

MARIA'S BANDERA ITALIANA (MARIA'S ITALIAN FLAG)

Serves 4–6

My 80-year-old Italian mother-in-law Maria Frisina makes wonderful rustic Calabrian food but also this easy and light vegetarian alternative to traditional lasagne.

INGREDIENTS

Sauce
1 large onion, finely sliced
olive oil
1 garlic clove (or to taste), crushed
400 g can diced tomatoes
700 ml bottle tomato passata

1 bunch English spinach
500 g fresh ricotta
3 garlic cloves, crushed
2 tablespoons olive oil
2 tablespoons cheese, grated
1 fresh Lebanese bread

METHOD

Preheat the oven to 180°C.

Lightly fry the onions in olive oil until soft, then add the garlic. Cook gently. Add the tomatoes and passata, bring to the boil then reduce the heat and simmer for 15 minutes.

Trim the spinach and steam the leaves. Squeeze out excess moisture and chop coarsely. Combine the spinach, ricotta, garlic, olive oil and cheese in a large bowl and mix well. Place a couple of ladles of sauce over the bottom of a baking dish. Open the bread on one side and place onto the sauce in the dish. Spoon the ricotta filling into the bread. Close the bread, and cover with the remaining sauce. Bake for 30 minutes. Serve with a green salad.

Christine Frisina, Mosman, NSW

MACARONI CHEESE
Serves 4

This is one of my favourite recipes because everyone seems to like it and I can make it quickly and easily if unexpected guests arrive; it is also a fantastic 'meal stretcher'. It can be made in the microwave and then browned under a griller or in the oven for the last few minutes (even better for really unexpected and/or late guests).

INGREDIENTS

150g short pasta (macaroni, penne, tubes, bows)
olive oil spray
2 tablespoons butter, melted
2 tablespoons plain flour
couple drops Tabasco sauce
1 teaspoon mustard (powder or prepared)
pinch of nutmeg, grated or ground
2 cups (500 ml) milk, gently warmed
½ cup (50 g) finely grated parmesan cheese
½ cup (60 g) grated good cheddar cheese
3 bacon rashers, diced
3 spring onions, sliced finely
breadcrumbs and extra grated parmesan cheese to top

METHOD

Preheat the oven to 180°C. Spray a 6-cup capacity ovenproof dish lightly with oil.

Cook the pasta according to packet directions. Meanwhile, combine the butter, flour, Tabasco, mustard and nutmeg in a saucepan. Slowly add the milk, stirring all the time. Cook over medium heat, stirring until bubbly and thickened. Season with salt and pepper, then add the cheeses and remove from the heat.

Cook the bacon and onion in a frying pan until softened.

Combine the pasta, bacon, onion and sauce in a bowl. Pour into the prepared dish. Top with the breadcrumbs and extra parmesan. Bake until heated and bubbly.

Tuck in with a green salad and some crusty bread, yum!

Cathy Noone, Warracknabeal, VIC

PASTA PIE
Serves 4–6

Since he was a toddler, my son Hugh has loved this dish and gave it its name. He is now a wonderful 20-year-old cook and pasta enthusiast. What I love about this recipe is that you can add whatever leftovers you have in the fridge to the pasta, egg and milk base, to come up with your own exotic variation and clean out the fridge at the same time. It is also great eaten cold for outdoor lunches or picnics.

INGREDIENTS

250g small pasta such as macaroni
200g bacon rashers, trimmed of fat and cut into small pieces
1 onion, chopped
4 spring onions, chopped
6 semi-dried tomatoes, drained and chopped
½ cup (60 g) grated tasty cheese
½ cup (50 g) grated parmesan cheese
5 eggs
2 cups (500 ml) milk
fresh herbs from your garden such as basil, oregano or thyme
sea salt and freshly ground pepper

Method

Preheat the oven to 180°C. Grease an 8-cup capacity ovenproof pie plate or casserole dish.

Cook the pasta in salted boiling water until just cooked. Drain and place into the prepared dish. Arrange the pasta so that it covers the base of the plate and is thicker at the edge like a piecrust.

Heat a non-stick frying pan. Fry the bacon, onion and spring onions for 2–3 minutes. Add the semi-dried tomatoes. Sprinkle the bacon mixture over the pasta and top with the grated cheeses.

Beat the eggs and milk together. Add the chopped herbs and salt and pepper to taste. Pour over the pasta.

Bake for 35–40 minutes until the filling sets and begins to brown.

Serve warm with a green salad with balsamic dressing and crusty bread.

Note: You can use a combination of pasta types if you want to use up the 'ends'. To vary the recipe you can replace the bacon with salmon (freshly cooked or canned), vary the cheese types (add some pieces of bocconcini, fabulous) or replace some of the milk with natural yoghurt or ricotta cheese.

Janice Sangster, Penshurst, NSW

SOPHIE'S PIZZA ROLL
Serves 8–12

In 1997 I took a trip back to Lebanon to visit my family. On this occasion we were holding a family gathering and I was asked to make pizza. Due to the large number of guests I didn't think this would be practical, so I had the idea to turn the pizza into 'pizza roll'. Well, it was a hit — and has been ever since — and has subsequently been dubbed Sophie's Pizza Roll.

INGREDIENTS

Dough

3 cups (450 g) plain flour, sifted

½ cup (125 ml) warm water

¼ cup (60 ml) warm milk

¼ cup (60 ml) olive oil

1 sachet dried yeast

1 teaspoon salt

1 teaspoon sugar

Filling

1½ cups (375 ml) tomato pasta sauce thickened slightly with sundried tomato tapenade or tomato paste

250 g mozzarella cheese, grated

250 g tasty cheese, grated

½ green capsicum, thinly sliced

½ red capsicum, thinly sliced

250 g mushrooms, sliced

1 large red onion, thinly sliced

200 g leg ham, thinly sliced

100 g salami

½ cup (70 g) Spanish olives, sliced

handful basil leaves

olive oil, for brushing

dried oregano, sesame seeds, poppy seeds

METHOD

To make the dough, make a well in the centre of the flour (in a large bowl or on a work surface). Add the water, milk and oil to the well and sprinkle the yeast, salt and sugar over the flour. Slowly mix together until it forms a dough. If it is too dry add more water and if it is too wet add a little more flour. The end result is that the dough should be nice and moist but leave your hands clean when kneading. Place the dough into a clean, lightly oiled bowl and cover with plastic wrap. Put in a warm place for about 30 minutes, until it doubles in size.

Preheat the oven to 220°C. Line baking trays with baking paper.

Divide the dough into 4 equal portions. Lightly flour the bench and roll each portion out as thinly as possible to a round pizza base.

To make the filling, spread tomato sauce over the base, leaving a 1 cm border around the edge. Sprinkle with most of the cheese. As this recipe will make at least 4 pizza rolls you can vary the filling of each to make vegetarian pizza rolls, or meat and vegetable combinations. Just be sure not to over fill each one as it will make the rolling difficult. Top the filling with remaining cheese and the fresh basil leaves.

Starting at one end, roll the pizza as tightly as possible until you get a long tight log. Fold the ends under and place onto a tray. Brush the top with oil and then sprinkle with either oregano, or the sesame or poppy seeds to help identify the filling. Score 6–8 evenly spaced diagonal slits across the top of the roll. Bake for about 20 minutes, until brown. Remove and cool before slicing into individual portions.

Enjoy!

Sophie Merheb, Peakhurst, NSW

PIPPA'S PASTIES
Makes about 12

These pasties are a connecting thread between many wonderful memories from my childhood. Beach picnics, bush excursions, autumn rambles for blackberries and mushrooms, all with family and friends.

The smell of them emerging golden from the wood-fired oven in our shack on Bruny Island, when we were all so sick of the fresh fish and crayfish we mainly lived on while on holiday there.

The day son number two gobbled 12 surreptitiously just prior to a winter swimming carnival and swam his best ever time! Two records in one day!

In my early adult years when I made them for my own family, I'd get mum over to help because only she seemed able to get the flavour right. This prompted stories from Mum's childhood, of helping her grandmother make pasties for her shop while staying with her on holiday, and what Ulverstone was like in the early nineteen twenties.

INGREDIENTS

Shortcrust pastry
125 g butter
125 g beef dripping
125 g lard
500 g plain flour, sifted
1 teaspoon salt
1 teaspoon cream of tartar
iced water with a squeeze of lemon juice added

Filling
1.5 kg potatoes
3 large onions
½ turnip
3 medium carrots

500 g minced beef
2 tablespoons Worcestershire sauce
2 tablespoons tomato sauce
sea salt and freshly ground pepper
water or egg wash to brush

METHOD

Preheat the oven to 210°C.

To make the shortcrust pastry, rub the fats into the dry ingredients then mix with enough water and lemon juice to make a firm pastry. Knead briefly on a lightly floured board, taking care not to overwork the dough. Place into a freezer bag or cover with plastic wrap and put into the refrigerator to rest while you make the filling.

Peel all the vegetables and chop coarsely. If you do this in a food processor, be sure to keep the vegetables a little chunky for a good texture. Combine promptly with the meat and sauces to limit the browning of the potatoes. Season with salt and pepper. Depending on the vegetables used and the time taken to finish the pasties, quite a lot of juice can gather in the bowl. Just avoid this when filling the pasties.

Roll out the pastry and cut into rounds. A saucer makes a good lady-like sized pastie for smaller appetites, a bread and butter plate or small dinner plate makes a more generous sized pastie.

Place a spoonful of filling onto the centre of the pastry round. Be as generous as the size will allow; they need to be as full as possible without making them impossible to mould. Brush around the edge of the pastry with a water or egg wash, then crimp the edges together over the top of the filling, fluting the pastry edges firmly between your fingers right from the top down to the pastry board, so no filling escapes in the baking.

Place onto a non-stick oven tray, brush with the egg or water wash and cook for about 30 minutes. Then reduce the heat to 180°C for a further 20 minutes or so. Remove when golden.

Note: These freeze and reheat well, and are great served with a spicy tomato relish.

Di Ayers, Campania, TAS

Broad Bean, Tomato and Pumpkin Soup

Serves 6

I love food and I love to cook! I love the Australian lifestyle and the fusion of cultures, flavours, dramatic and subtle environments, and the influence this has over the food Australia produces. From the much loved recipes of home, passed on from Mum and Nanna (invariably with an influence from another culture), to the unique and cutting edge cuisine our fabulous Australian chefs produce, I find this inspiring and I am addicted to experimentation with the flavours and textures of food. Healthy, fresh, seasonal and simple; this is my mantra. To combine a love of gardening with cooking fresh ingredients gives me endless pleasure.

Ingredients

1 large onion
3–4 garlic cloves
1 tablespoon butter
3 tablespoons olive oil
700g dried broad (fava) beans, soaked overnight and peeled
2 x 400 g cans diced Roma tomatoes
500 g butternut pumpkin, peeled and chopped
4 cups (1 L) fresh chicken stock or pre-packaged salt reduced chicken
    stock
small handful fresh thyme leaves and soft stems
sea salt and freshly ground pepper
parmesan cheese, extra thyme and fresh bread to serve

METHOD

Finely chop the onion and garlic. Heat the butter and oil in large heavy bottomed saucepan over medium high heat. Add the onion and cook until transparent but not brown. Add the garlic and cook for one minute while stirring.

Add the broad beans, tomatoes, pumpkin and stock, stir to combine. Add the thyme and season with salt and freshly ground black pepper to taste. Bring just to the boil, then reduce the heat and simmer for 45 minutes, or until the beans are cooked but still hold their shape.

Sprinkle with fresh thyme and serve with freshly grated parmesan cheese and slices of a heavy, good-quality bread like sourdough or pane de casa.

Note: You can use an organic herbed seasoning salt if you like.

Rebekah Raymond, Roseville Chase, NSW

Spicy butternut soup
Serves 4

This is my mother's recipe. The flavour improves with keeping for a day or two, but don't freeze it.

Ingredients

3 tablespoons butter
2 onions, chopped
2 cups (300 g) diced butternut pumpkin
1 Granny Smith apple, peeled and chopped
3 tablespoons plain flour
2 teaspoons curry powder
pinch ground nutmeg
3 cups (750 ml) chicken stock
1½ cups (375 ml) milk
grated rind and juice of 1 orange
parsley and cream, if desired
sea salt, freshly ground pepper and sugar to taste

Method

Melt the butter in a saucepan and sauté the onions until soft. Add the pumpkin and apple, sauté for 3 minutes. Add the flour, curry powder and nutmeg, stir well.

Add the stock, milk, orange rind and juice. Bring to the boil, reduce the heat and simmer slowly for 15–20 minutes until the pumpkin and apple are tender.

Cool, then purée in a blender or food processor until smooth. Add the parsley or cream, if desired. Season with salt, pepper and a pinch of sugar to taste. Serve hot or cold.

Maureen Glendining, Wagga Wagga, NSW

CHLODNIK (BARBIE SOUP)
Serves 4–6

Imagine this at a garden party on a hot summery evening or at a picnic on the beach. You won't believe it, but this dish will even be a hit the kids' parties! My 5-year-old daughter calls this treat 'Barbie Soup', because of its beautiful bright pink colour. Whenever I have the occasion to delight with Chlodnik (pronounced whodnick), I feel a connection with my roots. A journey back to my Eastern European childhood, filled with inspiring food and people. It's amazing how significant a role food plays in our life.

INGREDIENTS
3 Lebanese cucumbers, seeded and cubed
3 medium tomatoes, cubed
2 medium beetroot, cooked, peeled and cubed
1 small red capsicum, cubed
1 small green capsicum, cubed
1 bunch small red radishes, cubed
1 kg natural European style yoghurt
sea salt and freshly ground pepper
handful of chopped chives, dill and flat leaf parsley
12 small potatoes, halved and steamed with skins on
4 hardboiled eggs

METHOD
Combine the cucumbers, tomatoes, beetroot, capsicum and radish in a large bowl. Pour the yoghurt over, add ¾ of the herb mix and season with salt and pepper to taste. Stir all the ingredients gently, then refrigerate for 10 minutes. Serve Chlodnik over the steamed potatoes, topped with quartered hard boiled eggs and the remaining herbs.

Asia Aubert, Para Hills West, SA

Zucchini Soup (Green Soup)

Serves 4

My husband and I have been growing our own vegetables for many years as we believe that fresh ingredients are the secret to good and healthy eating. Good quality food needs little embellishment and stands on its own. Home grown produce has a great distinctive flavour and our tomatoes rarely need even salt and pepper.

Of course we have a surplus at times and I find this zucchini soup recipe helps to clear the decks! I enjoy sharing my recipes with friends, and also the glut of garden produce.

I must admit that the kitchen is my first priority after being away from home on holidays. I much prefer home cooking to restaurant meals.

INGREDIENTS

2 or 3 (900 g) zucchini, cut into chunks
1 small onion, diced
1 small potato, diced
good bunch of parsley
handful of mint
4 cups (1 L) chicken stock
1 dessertspoon powdered milk or a dollop of cream
sea salt and freshly ground pepper

METHOD

Put all the ingredients except powdered milk or cream into a large saucepan. Bring to the boil, then reduce the heat and simmer for about an hour. Remove from the heat and cool before blending to a purée. Add either the powdered milk or the cream and season with salt and pepper.

This soup is delicious either hot or cold. It freezes well, too.

Coral Whiting, Henty, NSW

GAZPACHO

Serves 6

This is a great summer entree, or a refreshing summer lunch combined with a crusty bread roll. It keeps well in the fridge for a few days, but is best eaten as soon as it is chilled.

INGREDIENTS

4 cups (1 L) tomato juice (canned or bottled)
1 Lebanese cucumber, finely diced
1 green capsicum, finely diced
1 red capsicum, finely diced
1 onion, peeled and finely chopped
1–2 garlic cloves, finely chopped
2 stalks celery, finely diced
1 carrot, grated
1 tablespoon chopped parsley
1 tablespoon chopped mint or basil
1 dessertspoon olive oil
1 dessertspoon white vinegar
½ teaspoon of chilli powder, or to taste
1 dessertspoon Worcestershire sauce (or ground black pepper to taste)
a few pine nuts, optional
chives, slivers or lemon and a few ice cubes, to garnish

METHOD

For a smooth soup, combine all the ingredients in a blender and process until pureed. Alternatively, mix all the ingredients together, stir to combine. Chill and serve with garnish of chives, slivers of lemon and a few ice cubes.

I prefer the unpureed soup, as it is refreshing and satisfyingly crunchy.

Note: If preferred you can use 500 g pureed fresh tomatoes with 2 cups (500 ml) of water, instead of the tomato juice, but this takes additional time. Other garnishes may include chopped herbs, sliced tomatoes and olives.

Stella Klepper, Coolah, NSW

HADDOCK KEDGEREE
Serves 4

My wife Gwen was born during the depression in 1935. During her schooling through the war years of the 1940s she was taught the basics of cooking by her grandmother, a shearer's cook. By an early age Gwen had learned the value of skilful, economical food preparation. A milliner by trade and married at 18, Gwen pursued her quest for cooking excellence. She learned both sweet making and cake decorating and conducted a successful cake decorating business from home. Gwen raised 3 children and 2 grandchildren. Sadly, after surviving 9 years with inoperable breast cancer, she died in 2004.

INGREDIENTS
½ cup (100 g) white rice
500 g smoked haddock (or smoked cod)
3 hard boiled eggs
75 g butter
1 tablespoon lemon juice
⅓ cup chopped parsley.

METHOD
Boil the rice for 12 minutes and drain. Place the haddock into a saucepan and cover with water. Bring to the boil, reduce the heat and simmer until tender. Drain well then flake the flesh, removing any bones. Peel the hard boiled eggs, chop two of them and slice the other.

Melt the butter in a saucepan, add the haddock and rice. Stir in the chopped eggs and heat thoroughly. Add the lemon juice and half the parsley.

Serve on large warm platter garnished with the sliced egg and sprinkled with remaining parsley.

Keith Holle, Caringbah, NSW

PEACHY CHICKEN SALAD
Serves 4

Peachy chicken salad is always on the list of favourite foods when my now adult children come home for Christmas. We live in the Goulburn Valley and are fortunate to enjoy the variety of delicious peaches grown here during summer. This recipe is quick and easy to make at home and fantastic to take on a picnic — just take the chicken, marinated peaches and lettuce in 3 separate containers in a cool pack and toss together at serving time. We have a walnut orchard at Katunga and I love to use fresh walnuts and walnut oil in my recipes.

INGREDIENTS
1 BBQ chicken
3 ripe yellow peaches
1 garlic clove, crushed
1 teaspoon grainy mustard or Dijon mustard
1 tablespoon sugar
1 tablespoon white wine vinegar
4 tablespoons walnut oil
1 tablespoon chopped parsley
large handful of lettuce leaves, to serve (butter or mignonette)
½ cup (50 g) walnut halves

METHOD
Remove the meat and skin from the chicken and tear into large chunks. Peel the peaches, remove the stones and cut into thick slices. Place the garlic, mustard, sugar, vinegar, oil and parsley into a jar and shake well to combine. Pour over the peaches and marinate in the fridge for 30 minutes. At serving time add the chicken to the peaches, toss together and arrange on a bed of lettuce leaves in a bowl. Sprinkle with the walnuts. Serve with crusty warm bread.

Beth Jackman, Katunga, VIC

MAIN MEALS

HOT SOUR SEAFOOD SOUP

Serves 4

Every summer our family gathered together at Rock Cottage, our holiday home on Kangaroo Island. The holiday was spent yabbying in the dam at Little Cuttlefish Farm, clambering down the cliffs to fish from Snapper Point, catching squid from the Penneshaw jetty, attempting to catch crayfish in the cray pot and utilising the deliciously fresh and aromatic herbs from Rock Cottage.

Jon, a fabulous cook, decided that a Thai style soup would be perfect with these fresh ingredients, and delicious on a warm evening. It was another stunning meal enjoyed on the lawns of Rock Cottage.

INGREDIENTS

4 tablespoons tom yum paste
6 cups (1.5 L) crayfish stock (see below), prawn or fish stock
4 kaffir lime leaves, finely chopped
1 red chilli, seeded and sliced
2 stalks lemon grass, very thinly sliced
1 small whole squid, cleaned and sliced into 5 mm strips
125 g fish fillets, cubed
125 g raw yabbies, shelled
2 spring onions, finely sliced
1 tablespoon lime or lemon juice
2 tomatoes, diced
1 handful fresh coriander

Method

Combine the tom yum paste and stock in a large saucepan and bring to the boil. Add the kaffir lime leaves, chilli and lemon grass and simmer for 15 minutes.

Add the squid, fish and yabbies and simmer for a further 5 minutes, until the fish and squid turn white and the yabbies turn pink. Stir in the spring onions, lime juice and tomatoes. Serve in bowls garnished with fresh coriander.

Note: To make crayfish stock, bring 4 L of cold water to the boil. Add 1 peeled and sliced carrot, 2 sliced stalks of celery, 4 bay leaves, a bouquet garni, 3 garlic cloves, 1 peeled and quartered onion, 2 teaspoons peppercorns, 1 tablespoon sea salt and a large crayfish shell. Return to the boil, then lower heat, cover and simmer for about 45 minutes. Strain and use immediately or store in refrigerator for up to 3 days, or in freezer for 2–3 months.

Pip Souter, Penneshaw, SA

PASTA MARINARA
Serves 2–4

This dish came about when my cheeky husband said he felt like pasta marinara for lunch. We were at our beach house, so I suggested he throw the crab pots in while I did a pantry search! I thawed out some prawns, he caught the crab, and 30 minutes later we had a beer and blissed out! I thought the dish was too delicious to keep to myself. Enjoy!

INGREDIENTS

4 tablespoons olive oil
2 anchovies
1 brown onion, diced
½ teaspoon ground cloves
½ teaspoon ground nutmeg
½ teaspoon ground paprika
2 x 400g cans diced tomatoes
2 teaspoons sugar
sea salt and freshly ground pepper
2 or 3 crabs
500 g pasta
8–12 raw prawns, peeled and deveined
⅓ cup (80 ml) white wine
chopped fresh basil, to taste

METHOD

Heat half the olive oil in a saucepan, and cook the anchovies until dissolved. Add the onion and sauté for a few minutes, until soft. Add the spices to the onions before adding the tomatoes and sugar. Season with sea salt and black pepper.

Blanch the crabs in a large saucepan of boiling water. Remove crabs and run under cold water. Clean and break in half, then half again. Return the water to the boil and cook the pasta according to packet directions, or until al dente.

Meanwhile, heat the remaining oil in a frying pan. Add the prawns and crabs and fry for 5 minutes. Remove the seafood from the frying pan and add to the sauce. Leave the frying pan on high heat and pour in the wine. Stir well then add to the tomato sauce. Add the basil and bring to a simmer.

Drain the pasta (but don't rinse). Place the pasta into serving bowls and spoon the sauce over.

Julie Nolan, Attadale, WA

PUMPKIN AND PINE NUT RISOTTO
Serves 6

I love to cook but don't have a lot of time as a working single mum, so I like to cook things that are quick and easy like stir fries, or else use my slow cooker and do tagines and casseroles. This is one of our favourite recipes.

INGREDIENTS
1 tablespoon olive oil
1 onion, finely diced
1 garlic clove, finely chopped
3 cups (660 g) Arborio rice
½ cup (125 ml) white wine
6 cups (1.5 L) gently boiling chicken stock
1 tablespoon butter
handful grated parmesan cheese
freshly ground pepper
400 g Jap or butternut pumpkin, cut into 1.5 cm cubes and roasted
handful toasted pine nuts

METHOD
Heat the oil in a heavy based saucepan over a medium low heat. Add the onion and garlic and cook until translucent, but not browned. Add the rice, and stir until coated with the oil, then add the wine. Allow the rice to absorb most of the wine then add the stock one ladleful at a time. Stir constantly, allowing the rice to absorb most of the stock between each addition.

When the stock has been absorbed and the rice is creamy, add the butter and parmesan cheese, and season with pepper. Stir through well, then add the pumpkin and pine nuts. Cover and cook on low for 2–3 minutes. Remove from the heat, stir well and serve with a leafy salad and crusty bread.

Dr Deirdre Marshall, Stratford, VIC

SALMON PATTIES

Serves 4

This is a family favourite and any slightly oily fish may be used. If fresh fillets are unavailable, canned Australian salmon or tuna may be substituted.

INGREDIENTS

4 salmon fillets, skinned and boned
4 medium potatoes, steamed and mashed
1 large onion, finely chopped
1 cup (150 g) frozen baby peas, steamed
2 tablespoons finely chopped parsley
sea salt and freshly ground pepper
2 eggs, lightly beaten
2 cups (200 g) dried breadcrumbs
olive oil

METHOD

Steam the salmon and flake it with a fork while still hot. In a bowl, mix together the hot salmon, mashed potato, onion, peas and parsley. Season with salt and pepper then leave to cool for 10 minutes.

Form the mixture into eight patties. Dip into the beaten egg and roll in the breadcrumbs, shaking off the excess.

Heat the oil in a large frying pan and cook the patties until the coating is golden brown and crispy. Serve warm or cold with sweet chilli sauce or tomato dipping sauce, and lemon wedges.

Joy Seevers, Lakes Entrance, VIC

STEAMED WHOLE FISH WITH GINGER SAUCE

Serves 4

INGREDIENTS

1 medium carrot
1 stalk celery
1 green capsicum
1 red capsicum
4 very fresh small whole bream
1 tablespoon olive oil

Ginger sauce
1 tablespoon grated fresh ginger
2 teaspoons sugar
2 teaspoons dry sherry
1 tablespoon light soy sauce
2 teaspoons cornflour
1 cup (250 ml) water
3 spring onions, sliced diagonally

METHOD

Cut the carrot, celery and capsicums into thin strips. Boil, steam or microwave briefly until just tender, drain well. Fill the cavity of each fish with the vegetables, and secure the openings with toothpicks. Brush the fish lightly with oil and place into a large steamer in a single layer. Cover and steam for 10 minutes, or until tender. Remove the toothpicks before serving.

To make the sauce, combine the ginger, sugar, sherry and soy sauce in a small saucepan. Blend the cornflour in a little of the water to make a smooth paste. Stir in with the remaining water. Stir over high heat until the mixture boils and thickens, then add the spring onions.

Serve the fish over rice, drizzled with the sauce.

Keith Holle, Caringbah, NSW

CHICKEN WITH TOMATO AND BASIL

Serves 4

On my way home from work, feeling tired, I was wondering what my family of four could have for dinner. I called in at the supermarket and came across the chicken legs. Armed with the other ingredients I created this recipe. It was quick to prepare and tasted great.

INGREDIENTS

8 chicken lovely legs (drumsticks without skin or tips)
¼ cup (35 g) plain flour
2–3 tablespoons olive oil
1 large onion, chopped
1 fat garlic clove, chopped
3 medium fresh tomatoes, peeled and chopped
sea salt and freshly ground pepper
3 tablespoons chopped basil

METHOD

Preheat the oven to 190°C.

Trim any sinew from the chicken. Place the legs into a plastic bag, add the flour and shake to coat. Heat 2 tablespoons of oil in large frying pan. When it is hot add the chicken legs and brown all over, adding extra oil if needed.

Transfer the chicken to a casserole dish. Add a small amount of oil to the frying pan and fry the onion and garlic until soft and transparent. Pour over the chicken. Scatter the chopped tomatoes over and season with a little salt and pepper. Cover and cook for one hour.

Serve two legs per person with the tomatoes and onions. Sprinkle over the basil. This is lovely with creamy mashed potato and a green vegetable.

Rosemarie Noakes, Chapman, ACT

CHICKEN WITH APRICOTS, CORIANDER AND CIDER
Serves 8

I first tried this recipe when I was cooking for a dinner party in Hampshire, England. It was a great success and everyone loved it. But what makes it all the more memorable to me is that when I came home to Australia I decided to make it for a friend of ours and his new fiancée. After spending time painstakingly trying to get this sour woman to talk, I'd decided that at least we could enjoy a good meal. She was such a rude person, who had no 'smile' lines whatsoever, for lack of smiling! With dinner on the table she piped up and said 'Well, Peter is allergic to nuts!' Strange thing is he never used to be!

INGREDIENTS
8 chicken breast fillets
sea salt and freshly ground pepper
2 tablespoons plain flour
25g butter
1 tablespoon olive oil
1 onion, chopped
1¼ cups (225 g) dried apricots, chopped
1 cup (100 g) walnut halves
2 teaspoons plain flour, extra
600 ml dry cider
600 ml chicken stock
fresh coriander
salt and pepper

METHOD

Preheat oven to 180°C.

Season the chicken and coat in the flour, shaking off any excess (reserve 2 teaspoons of flour). Heat the butter and oil in a frying pan, then add the chicken and cook until browned. Place the chicken into a large, shallow ovenproof dish.

Add the onion to the pan and fry until golden. Add the apricots and walnuts and fry for one minute. Stir the extra flour into the pan and cook for 2 minutes while stirring. Pour in the cider and stock, and bring to the boil.

Remove from the heat, add salt and pepper to taste. Pour over the chicken and sprinkle with coriander, reserving a little to garnish. Cover, and bake for 30 minutes.

Serve garnished with coriander.

Mesha Hall, Wagin, WA

ROAST CHICKEN WITH LEMON MYRTLE STUFFING

Serves 4

This recipe is a result of a passion I have for gardening and growing Australian native plants in our modestly sized backyard. The lemon myrtle is one of my favourite plants as it is so versatile and pungent in smell and taste. A little goes a long way. If you do have the luxury of owning such a plant, you may substitute fresh leaves for dried. This recipe consists of everyday ingredients found in the pantry and is easily prepared. In summertime I like to lighten the stuffing up by adding fresh basil and parsley.

INGREDIENTS

⅓ cup (60 g) couscous
½ teaspoon ground lemon myrtle, or 8 fresh leaves
½ cup (125 ml) boiling water
5 dried baby figs, cut into quarters
2 tablespoons raisins
3 tablespoons slivered almonds
5 dried apricot halves, chopped
5 prunes, pitted and roughly chopped
1 tablespoon chopped parsley (optional)
1 small handful basil leaves (optional)
salt and pepper, to taste
1 size 14 chicken
olive oil
extra lemon myrtle
sea salt flakes

METHOD

Preheat the oven to 180°C.

Place the couscous and lemon myrtle into a bowl. Add the boiling water, cover tightly and stand for 5 minutes. Uncover and fluff up the grains with a fork. Add the figs, raisins, almonds, apricots and prunes to the couscous (along with the herbs if using), and mix well. Season with salt and pepper.

Wash the chicken and pat dry. Fill the cavity with the stuffing. Lightly oil the chicken and season with more lemon myrtle and sea salt flakes. Bake for 1½ hours, until cooked through.

Note: Ground lemon myrtle is available from good health food stores. Substitute with finely grated lemon rind if unavailable. If using fresh leaves, discard after cooking as you would with bay leaves.

Martina Zeitler, Elsternwick, VIC

MOROCCAN CHICKEN SALAD WITH GRILLED HALOUMI

Serves 4

This recipe comes from my recent interest in Moroccan flavours and a holiday on Kangaroo Island, where I discovered minted haloumi. Home style cooking for me is all about fresh ingredients, carefully teamed for balance and flavour. Fortunately our palates have become much 'lighter', inviting an array of options for quick and healthy eating using all kinds of flavours from across the globe.

INGREDIENTS

4 skinless chicken thigh fillets, halved
1 packet (180 g) haloumi cheese, cut into 8 (5 mm thick) pieces
Greek style yoghurt, to serve
freshly ground pepper
olive oil, extra

Marinade
½ cup (125 g) plain Greek style yoghurt
1½ teaspoons ground cumin
½ teaspoon curry powder
½ teaspoon ground coriander
1 tablespoon chopped mint
1 tablespoon chopped flat leaf parsley
1 teaspoon ground sumac
1 teaspoon brown sugar
juice of ½ lemon
1 garlic clove, crushed

Salad

3 tablespoons extra virgin olive oil
1½ tablespoons red wine vinegar
2 handfuls rocket leaves
½ carrot, peeled lengthways into curls
1 Lebanese cucumber, cut into thin strips
½ cup (80 g) canned chickpeas, rinsed and drained
¼ small red onion, finely sliced
chopped mint

METHOD

Mix the marinade ingredients together in a ceramic or glass dish. Add the chicken pieces and turn until well coated. Cover and refrigerate for at least 2 hours, or overnight.

For the salad, combine the olive oil and red wine vinegar to make a dressing. Place the rest of the salad ingredients into a bowl and toss through the dressing.

Preheat a BBQ plate to medium heat.

Cook the marinated chicken, turning frequently, for about 8 minutes, until cooked through and lightly browned. Grill the haloumi slices on the BBQ plate for about 1 minute each side until golden brown.

Place some of the salad in the middle of each plate and top with 2 grilled chicken pieces and 2 slices of haloumi. Serve with a dollop of Greek style yoghurt and freshly ground black pepper. Drizzle with a little extra olive oil if you like.

Lisa Thompson-Gordon, Footscray, VIC

CLASSIC FORTY CLOVES CHICKEN
Serves 6

I was one of the members of the Lombardy Elephants Artist Group, who once a month got together and produced some fantastic art. I decided to cook this recipe at one of our monthly gatherings for everyone to taste. People were dubious at first, however once they tasted the chicken they were amazed at how deliciously sweet the garlic had become.

INGREDIENTS
1 whole chicken, cut into pieces
40 garlic cloves
4 stalks celery, cut in 1-inch pieces
1 zucchini, sliced
1 red capsicum, diced
1 lemon, halved
½ cup (125 ml) dry white wine
¼ cup (60 ml) dry vermouth
1 teaspoon dried oregano
2 teaspoons dried basil
6 sprigs parsley, minced
pepper

METHOD
Preheat the oven to 190°C.

Place the chicken pieces into a large shallow baking pan, skin side up. Place the garlic, celery, zucchini and capsicum in and around the chicken. Squeeze the juice from the lemon over the chicken, then cut the lemon into pieces and add to the pan.

Drizzle with the wine and vermouth, and sprinkle with the herbs and pepper. Cover with foil and bake for 40 minutes. Remove the foil and bake an additional 15 minutes. Season with salt and pepper to taste.

Wendy Turley, Bealiba, VIC

HOI SIN STEAMED CHICKEN
Serves 4

This recipe came about while waiting for garden rubbish to finish burning. In our Land Rover days we enjoyed this menu when out camping. Once prepared, the meat can be wrapped in foil and thrown on a fire or grilled on a BBQ. We usually have it cooked in the oven.

INGREDIENTS
6 skinless chicken thigh fillets
2 teaspoons hoisin sauce
1 onion, sliced into rings but not pulled apart
a little water
sea salt and freshly ground pepper

METHOD
Preheat the oven to 180°C.

Remove all the fat and traces of bone from the chicken. Cut two of the fillets in half. Open each whole fillet out so that one slice of onion can be laid inside. Roll up each whole fillet with a half fillet, enclosing the onion. Secure with a tooth pick if you like. Spread the hoisin sauce over the chicken. Either wrap each roll in foil, or wrap the lot in foil, or place them all into a covered casserole dish. Add a tiny amount of water to each package so that the chicken cooks in the steam, and season with salt and pepper to taste. Cook in the oven for 40 minutes.

You could cook the foil-wrapped chicken on the BBQ for about 25 to 30 minutes. When camping, cook in the not too hot coals of a fire for 15 to 20 minutes. When opening the parcels or casserole dish, beware of scalding steam.

Enjoy with minted new potatoes, and carrots and peas. Use the spare juice as a thin gravy.

John and Esther Cribbes, Sale, VIC

STIR-FRIED HONEY CHICKEN
Serves 4–6

The uni student's recipe for Mum. After leaving home for uni, each child rang with, 'How do you do this?', or 'What was the recipe for that?' It was a proud day when my son presented me with his home-cooked stir fry which we enjoyed at his first house with other students, and he handed over the recipe.

INGREDIENTS

1 tablespoon oil
1 onion, cut into wedges
2 chicken breast fillets, sliced
500 g broccoli, chopped
150 g snow peas
1 red capsicum, sliced
⅓ cup (80 ml) water
¼ cup (60 ml) lemon juice
2 tablespoons honey
2 teaspoons soy sauce
3 teaspoons cornflour

METHOD

Heat the oil in a wok or pan. Add the onion and stir fry until soft. Add the chicken and stir fry over high heat until tender. Add the broccoli, snow peas and capsicum and stir fry for 1 minute.

Combine the water, juice, honey, soy sauce and cornflour. Add to the wok and stir until the mixture boils and thickens. Serve with boiled rice.

Kate Norman, Edenhope, VIC

CRISPY TWICE-COOKED BBQ DUCK RISOTTO
Serves 6

I am so passionate about food, dining out and experiencing new tastes. I would love to submit my risotto recipe for a home-cooked meal. You can enjoy it with your family on a Sunday evening with a glass of red, or you can present it in a way that will 'wow' all your friends at a Saturday night dinner party.

INGREDIENTS
Stock
1 BBQ duck
1 carrot, chopped
1 onion, chopped
2 stalks celery, chopped

100 ml olive oil
30 g butter
1 brown onion, chopped
1 garlic clove, chopped
1½ cups (330 g) Arborio rice
200 ml dry white wine
150 ml kecap manis (sweet soy sauce)
150 g mixed mushrooms, lightly sautéed in oil
2 spring onions, chopped
sesame oil, to garnish
1 sheet nori (dried seaweed), finely sliced
150 g parmesan cheese, finely grated

Method

Remove the meat from the duck bones (keeping the breast intact). To make the stock, combine the bones and the chopped vegetables in a large saucepan, and add 2 litres of water. Bring to the boil, then reduce the heat and simmer until reduced by a quarter (to 1.5 L). Strain the stock, discard the bones and vegetables. Return to the pan and keep at a simmer. Shred the duck meat (excluding the breast) and place onto a baking tray, with the breast skin side up.

Heat the oil and butter in a heavy based saucepan. Add the onion and cook over medium heat until soft. Add the garlic and rice, and cook until the rice has a transparent appearance. Add the wine and stir until absorbed. Add the stock 1 cup (250 ml) at a time, stirring until absorbed. Continue until all the stock has been added and absorbed.

Place the duck meat under a hot grill until it becomes crisp. Once crispy, cut each breast into 3 pieces. Add the kecap manis, mushrooms, spring onions and shredded duck meat to the risotto.

To make the parmesan biscuits, preheat the oven to 220°C, and line a baking tray with a sheet of baking paper. Make circles of grated parmesan cheese about 6 cm in diameter and 5 mm thick. Bake for 2–3 minutes until golden brown and bubbling. Remove and leave until cool and crisp.

To serve, pack the risotto into a bowl shaped cup and turn out onto a large white plate. Garnish with the crispy duck breast on top, drizzle a small amount of sesame oil around the plate and sprinkle with sliced nori. Serve with parmesan biscuits.

Note: BBQ duck is available from good Asian food shops or Chinese restaurants. Use a variety of mushrooms such as Swiss, button, field and shiitake.

Steve Shields, Morningside, QLD

STUFFED PORK FILLET
Serves 2

We headed off camping with a pork fillet, some prosciutto and mustard in the esky, to make our favourite dish. Alas, the key ingredient, the oven roasted capsicum, was at home in the fridge — so we improvised with what we had. Inspired by the complimentary flavours of our cheese, dried fruit and nut platter, we created a stuffed pork fillet with exquisite, exotic flavours that infused into the meat and lingered like those of a good red wine.

INGREDIENTS
400–500 g pork fillet
wholegrain honey mustard
creamy blue cheese
12–15 dried pitted dates, halved
8 thin slices prosciutto

METHOD
Preheat the oven to 180°C.

Cut the silvery membrane from the fillet to avoid curling and shrinkage. Butterfly the pork fillet and tenderise with a meat mallet. Fold in the thin ends to maintain an oblong shape and even thickness.

Spread a layer of honey mustard over the meat. Spread a little blue cheese onto each date, and place two rows of dates in the centre of the pork. Fold the meat to enclose the filling and make a neat sausage shape.

Overlap the slices of the prosciutto on a board. Place the pork on the middle of the prosciutto and fold the pieces over the meat. Roll the pork over so that the ends of the prosciutto are underneath. Place onto a baking tray and bake for 20 minutes, or put onto a hot BBQ and cook on low to medium heat for 20 minutes, turning occasionally.

Serve with a colourful tossed salad.

Charmaine and Greg Burton, Pooraka, SA

Pork fillet with avocado
Serves 4

Having a small orchard at Eumundi many years back, we had an abundance of avocados, limes and macadamias. When family and friends visited it was great to use the produce from the orchard. This recipe was always one of the favourites. To finish off the meal I always made a light lime soufflé.

Ingredients
2 medium pork fillets
2 teaspoons oil
2 small onions, finely chopped
150 g cream cheese
8 small button mushrooms
2 ripe avocados
⅔ cup (100 g) plain flour,
    seasoned with salt and pepper
2 eggs, lightly beaten
200 g crushed macadamia nuts
50 g clarified butter
1 lime, sliced

Sauce
150 g clarified butter
juice of 1 lime
3 sprigs fresh tarragon

Method

Preheat the oven to 180°C.

Trim the pork fillets, and cut each in half. Place between two pieces of plastic wrap and flatten carefully with a meat mallet. Set aside.

Heat the oil in a small pan and cook the onion until soft. Let cool, then blend with the cream cheese.

Blanch the mushrooms and set aside.

Lay the fillets out on a board. Place some cheese mixture in the centre of each fillet, add 2 mushrooms and a generous slice of avocado (keep remaining avocado for garnish). Roll the fillets carefully, enclosing the filling. Roll in seasoned flour, coat with beaten egg and then the macadamia nuts. Shallow fry in butter until golden brown, then transfer to an oven tray and bake for 5–10 minutes.

To prepare the sauce, heat the butter until just starting to brown, add the lime juice and tarragon while sizzling and serve immediately over the pork. Garnish with lime and avocado slices.

Joan Vincent, St Ives, NSW

PORK AND LYCHEE STIR-FRY

Serves 4

This recipe is tasty, healthy, colourful, and quick! Ideal for the 'working cook'.

INGREDIENTS

600 g pork, sliced or cubed
3 teaspoons Chinese five spice powder
½ cup (125 ml) soy sauce
¼ cup (60 ml) peanut oil
½ cup (60 g) chopped walnuts
565 g can lychees, drained (or equivalent fresh)
1 bunch bok choy, chopped

METHOD

Place the pork into a shallow ceramic or glass dish and add the five spice powder and soy sauce. Combine and marinate for at least one hour.

Heat the oil in a wok, and toss the walnuts until lightly toasted. Add the pork meat and stir fry until cooked. Add lychees and bok choy, and heat through.

Serve on a bed of noodles or rice.

Marilyn Crozier, Taree, NSW

PORK AND LEMON CASSEROLE
Serves 4–6

This has become a firm favourite with family and friends and over the years has evolved. It is a thoroughly yummy and hearty meal. There is only one problem with this recipe — there are never enough chops!

INGREDIENTS
1 tablespoon brown sugar
1 teaspoon salt
1 teaspoon pepper
½ cup (75 g) plain flour
6 pork loin chops
vegetable oil for frying
3 onions, sliced
1 green capsicum, sliced
1 red capsicum, sliced
1 large lemon, finely sliced

METHOD
Preheat the oven to 180°C.

Mix the sugar, salt, pepper and flour together. Dredge both sides of the pork chops with the flour and shake off any excess. Fry in a little oil until browned on both sides. Remove and place into a casserole dish. In the same pan, sauté the onion and capsicum until just tender. Place the onion mixture on top of chops.

Arrange the lemon slices on top, and pour in enough water to barely cover the chops. Cover and bake for 1–1½ hours or until the chops are very tender. Thicken if necessary. Serve with rice and vegetables for good colour contrast.

Ellen O'Dempsey, Helensburgh, NSW

PORK, POTATO AND SMOKED PAPRIKA PIE

Serves 6

*My four-year-old daughter calls this 'Dead Piggy in a Pie' —
she's recently learnt where meat comes from. I think 'Pork,
potato and smoked paprika pie' sounds much more delicious. I
first made this in August 2004. As usual, after creating
something worth making again, I struggled to remember what I
threw in, and scrawled it down on paper.*

*It's not a quick meal, but worth making when you have the
time.*

INGREDIENTS

2 tablespoons olive oil
1½ red onions, 1 finely diced, ½ thinly sliced
pinch of salt
2 tablespoons plain flour
1 teaspoon smoked sweet paprika
¼ teaspoon white pepper
½ teaspoon ground coriander
generous grating or pinch of nutmeg
500 g pork, cut into large cubes
4 small carrots, very finely diced
3 potatoes, coarsely grated
200 g mushrooms (Swiss brown or button), quartered
1–2 tablespoons fish sauce
¼ cup (60 ml) lemon juice
¼ cup (60 ml) chicken stock
3 teaspoons Dijon mustard
3 garlic cloves, crushed
2 pinches saffron threads
300 ml thickened cream
¼ cup chopped flat leaf parsley

2 sheets frozen puff pastry, thawed
milk (for brushing pastry)
sesame seeds
a little extra smoked paprika

METHOD
Preheat the oven to 170°C.

Heat the olive oil in a heavy based flameproof casserole dish. Cook the diced onions in olive oil with a pinch of sea salt until soft.

Combine the flour, paprika, pepper, coriander and nutmeg in a bowl. Dust the pork in the flour mixture and shake off the excess. Brown the pork in two batches with the cooked diced onion. Return all the pork to the pan.

Add the sliced onion, carrots, potato, mushrooms, fish sauce, lemon juice, stock, mustard, garlic, saffron and cream. Bring just to the boil, then reduce the heat and simmer gently for 5 minutes.

Wet and scrunch up a sheet of baking paper. Flatten out the paper, then press it down onto the surface of the mixture to keep moisture in. Cover with a lid. Bake for 1½ hours. Remove from the oven and stir in the parsley.

Increase the oven to 200°C. Transfer the mixture to a pie dish (or individual large ramekins). Cover with pastry, brush with milk, then sprinkle with sesame seeds and a little extra smoked paprika. Bake for about 20 minutes, until pastry is golden.

Lou Hendricks, Prospect, SA

MARINATED LAMB CUTLETS
Serves 4

INGREDIENTS
12 lamb cutlets, trimmed of fat
½ cup (125 ml) soy sauce
1 cup (250 ml) tomato sauce
1 cup (250 ml) sweet chilli sauce
1 cup (250 ml) Worcestershire sauce
½ cup (125 ml) BBQ sauce
1 cup (250 ml) honey
4 garlic cloves, crushed
1 teaspoon minced ginger

METHOD
Put the cutlets into a ceramic or glass mixing bowl. Add all the sauces, honey, garlic and ginger and mix well. Cover with foil or plastic wrap, put in the fridge and leave overnight.

Preheat a frying pan or BBQ to very hot. Drain the cutlets from the marinade, and cook for about 2 minutes each side. Serve with a tossed salad and garlic roasted potatoes, or steamed vegetables.

Note: To use the leftover marinade as a sauce, place into a saucepan and bring to the boil. Boil for 5 minutes, to kill any bacteria from the meat. This marinade is also very nice using pork spare ribs instead of lamb.

John Stanford, Inglewood, VIC

LAMB SHANKS
Serves 6

The story behind this recipe is that I had three boys, all of whom ate an enormous amount of meat 'What do you mean, this is vegetarian, where is the meat?!' I sometimes despaired of ever filling them up on my budget. After paying school fees, buying soccer boots, rugby boots, cricket sets and paying for school trips etc., there often wasn't the money for T-bone steak every night.

So, this casserole was developed and tried and demolished and became a much-loved dinner. Even now that our boys don't live with us, they demand this dinner on family nights.

INGREDIENTS
¼ cup (60 ml) olive oil
6 lamb shanks, cut through
1 large onion, chopped
3 carrots, chopped
3 parsnips, sliced
4 stalks of celery, sliced
400g can diced tomatoes
roughly chopped fresh herbs, such as rosemary, thyme and oregano
sea salt and freshly ground pepper
¼ cup (55 g) red lentils, optional
1 cup (250 ml) chicken stock
2 glasses (about 250 ml) good red wine
1 tablespoon cornflour
3 tablespoons tomato paste

METHOD

Preheat the oven to 150°C.

Heat the oil in a frying pan and cook the lamb shanks (in batches) until well browned. Transfer to a large casserole dish. In the same pan, brown the onion and add to the casserole, along with the carrot, parsnips and celery.

Add the tomatoes and herbs, season with salt and pepper, and add the lentils if you are using them. Pour the stock and wine into the frying pan. Dissolve the cornflour in ½ cup (125 ml) water and add to the pan with the tomato paste. Stir until thick and bubbling. Cook for 2 minutes.

Pour into the casserole, using a large spoon to evenly spread the sauce through the lamb and vegetables. Cover and bake for at least 3 hours, and up to 4 hours. Serve with mashed potato and green salad.

Dian Ball, Pyrmont, NSW

MUM'S SHEPHERD'S PIE
Serves 4

I grew up with this recipe and so have my children. I often put other vegetables such as leek or grated turnip in it. It is certainly very different to some Shepherd's Pies I have tasted.

INGREDIENTS

500 g lamb mince
1 large onion, finely chopped
2 stalks celery, finely chopped
2 carrots, peeled and finely chopped
2 parsnips, peeled and finely chopped
1 teaspoon ground allspice
1 tablespoon tomato paste
2 cups (500 ml) beef stock
1 bay leaf
sea salt and freshly ground pepper
1 kg potatoes, peeled, boiled and mashed

METHOD

Preheat the oven to 180°C.

Cook the mince in a non-stick frying pan until well browned. Discard the liquid. Add the onion, celery, carrot, parsnips and allspice; cook for 1 minute. Add the tomato paste, stock, bay leaf and salt and pepper. Bring to the boil, reduce the heat and simmer for 30 minutes.

Place into a greased pie dish and top with mashed potato. Bake until the potato browns on top. Serve with pumpkin and beans for a good colour combination.

Ellen O'Dempsey, Helensburgh, NSW

THE BEST MEAT PIE EVER!

Serves 4–6

After moving out of home and trying commercial meat pies for an easy dinner, I was disappointed with half-full pies of tasteless filling and gristly bits. It didn't take me long to have a go at making my own. I'm only at uni but love to feed people so this is a cheap and impressive meal. Be warned, once you have gone to the effort of making your own you'll never buy one from the freezer again!

INGREDIENTS

1 kg chuck steak, cubed
⅓ cup (50 g) plain flour, seasoned with salt and pepper
2–3 tablespoons oil
6 baby onions
small handful cubed speck or bacon
1 garlic clove, crushed (optional)
chopped chilli, to taste (optional)
4 cups (1 L) reduced salt beef stock
125 g button mushrooms
1–2 sheets frozen puff pastry, thawed
1 egg, lightly beaten

METHOD

Coat the meat in well seasoned flour, and shake off any excess.

Heat 1 tablespoon of the oil in a frying pan, and brown the meat in batches, adding 1 teaspoon of oil to the pan for each new batch. Set the browned meat aside. (Don't worry about the bits getting stuck and brown on the bottom. That is what makes the sauce thick and tasty!)

Cook the onions and speck in the same pan until the onions are brown and the speck has released its fat. You can also add garlic and chilli at this stage if you are in the mood.

Return the meat and any juices to the pan. Gradually add 1 cup of stock to the pan, scraping all the yummy bits off the bottom and stirring in all the floury bits to thicken the sauce.

Add another 2 cups of stock (reserve one). Bring just to the boil, then immediately reduce the heat to low. Simmer, partially covered, for about 2 hours, adding button mushrooms and a bit more stock after one hour. When the meat is falling apart and the gravy is thick, leave to cool.

Preheat the oven to 200°C.

Divide the mixture between ramekins and top with a circle of puff pastry. Brush the tops with egg and cut a cross in the tops. Bake for about 20 minutes, until the pastry is brown and crispy.

Michelle Davies, Glasshouse Mountains, QLD

GRANNY TUXEN'S SAVOURY MEAT PIE

Serves 6

This delicious recipe was given to my mother many years ago, by the mother of a dear friend. My sisters and I have cooked it for our families for over fifty years. It is truly comfort food.

INGREDIENTS

400 g beef or lamb mince (or leftover cold roast meat)
1 onion, chopped
4 bacon rashers, chopped
2 tablespoons plain flour
160 ml water, stock or gravy
½ cup chopped parsley
2 tablespoons tomato sauce
sea salt and freshly ground pepper
6 eggs
1 sheet frozen puff pastry, thawed
1 egg yolk

METHOD

Preheat the oven to 190°C. Grease a pie plate ot dish.

Mix all the ingredients except the eggs and pastry together, and season with salt and pepper. Make 6 hollows in the top of the meat mixture, and break the eggs into the hollows. Prick the yolks with a fork, sprinkle with salt and pepper.

Place the pastry sheet over the filling, pressing the edges over the sides. Trim and mark edges with a fork. Prick the top a few times and brush with the egg yolk mixed with a little water. Bake for 15 minutes, then reduce the heat to 165°C and cook for a further 30 minutes or until golden brown.

This is delicious hot or cold, which makes it great for a picnic. Serve with a green salad and a tomato and avocado salsa.

Noel Hayman, Walkerville, SA

GLORIA'S MEATLOAF

Serves 4–6

We moved from Sydney to a small rural community in Tasmania, where the nearest shops were a 70 km round trip. The warmth and generosity of our new neighbours was astounding. We received welcoming gifts of farm produce, advice and lots of help. So when I attended a fundraising luncheon and tasted this meatloaf, made by my neighbour Gloria, I knew that when I asked for the recipe it would be passed on to me without equivocation. It is a great standby when cooking from the freezer and store cupboard, good hot with gravy, cold with salad, or in sandwiches.

INGREDIENTS

1 kg good quality lean minced steak
1 cup (60 g) fresh breadcrumbs
¼ teaspoon ground pepper
1 medium onion, chopped
1 teaspoon dried mixed herbs
2 bacon rashers, chopped
30 g packet spring vegetable soup
1 cup (250 ml) evaporated milk

METHOD

Preheat the oven to 180°C.

Place all the ingredients into a large mixing bowl and mix until thoroughly combined. Lightly pack into a loaf tin.

Cook for 1 hour or until the loaf shrinks slightly from the sides. Serve hot or cold.

Frances Hillier, Woodsdale, TAS

Baked beef patties in sauce
Serves 4

I started cooking this recipe for my large family in the 1960s (I had five sons). I had collected recipes over a few years and then in April 1969 I wanted to teach myself how to type. So, on an old click clack typewriter, I very slowly typed these recipes into a little book which I still have. This recipe is very tasty, easy to cook and has never failed to please 'my boys'.

Ingredients

450 g minced topside or round steak
1 cup (60 g) fresh breadcrumbs
½ teaspoon each of salt and pepper
¼ cup chopped parsley
1 small onion, grated
1 egg, beaten
¼ cup (35 g) plain flour, seasoned with salt and pepper
1 cup (250 ml) stock or water
1 tablespoon Worcestershire sauce
2 tablespoons chutney or tomato sauce
1 tablespoon vinegar
1 level dessertspoon brown sugar
4 medium tomatoes, thickly sliced

Method

Put the minced steak, breadcrumbs, salt and pepper, parsley and onion into a large bowl. Add the egg and use your hands to evenly combine. Shape into 8 patties. Coat lightly in seasoned flour and shake off the excess.

Arrange the patties into a deep casserole or baking dish. Blend the stock (or water), sauces, vinegar and sugar. Pour over the patties. Allow to stand for 1 hour.

Preheat the oven to 200°C.

Turn the patties over and bake for 30 minutes. Remove from the oven, turn the patties over again and arrange the tomatoes over the top. Season with salt and pepper and bake for a further 20 minutes. Serve with mashed potato and steamed vegetables.

Note: Use breadcrumbs made from day-old bread rather than packaged dry breadcrumbs.

Lorraine Wyatt, Surfers Paradise, QLD

CORNED BEEF

Serves 4

One of my Mum's regularly cooked main courses — at least once or twice a fortnight — was corned beef, with spuds and overcooked cabbage. (It took me at least 25 years before I could face cabbage again, albeit cooked rather differently.) The sauce was tinned cream of celery soup.

After 20 years in Asia, I still hankered after some of the old Aussie favourites, but with a little more pizazz.

INGREDIENTS

1.5 kg (approx.) corned silverside, preferably the eye
1 large onion, coarsely chopped
2 stalks celery, cut into 5 cm pieces
1 large carrot, coarsely chopped
½ cup (90 g) shaved palm sugar
6 cups (1.5 L) dry white wine
2 cups (500 ml) light chicken stock
1 cup (250 ml) mirin or white wine vinegar
2 teaspoons black peppercorns
2 large potatoes, peeled and cut into quarters
8 chats potatoes, unpeeled
1 bunch baby (Dutch) carrots, scrubbed, green tops trimmed to 5 cm long
finely ground white pepper
30 g butter
½ cup flat leaf parsley
freshly ground black pepper
2 teaspoons Dijon mustard

METHOD

Remove all the excess fat and membrane from the meat. Cut off a small sliver of the meat, and chew (then spit out!) to check for saltiness. If only mildly salty, immerse in fresh water for 30 minutes. If very salty, immerse in fresh water (in the fridge) for up to 4 hours, changing the water several times.

Place the silverside into a large pot with the onion, celery, carrot, sugar, wine, stock, mirin and peppercorns. If the meat is not completely covered, add more stock or water. Bring to the boil, reduce the heat and simmer gently for 2½ hours.

Preheat the oven to 120°C.

Add the peeled potatoes, the chats and the baby carrots to the pot. Return to a low boil for 30 minutes, then remove from the heat and take out the baby carrots, the chats, and the peeled potatoes. Cover the pot and let stand.

Place the baby carrots and the chats into a casserole dish, and spoon over a couple of tablespoons of the cooking liquid. Sprinkle on some white pepper, dot with butter, cover and put in the oven to keep warm.

Put the remaining potatoes into a blender, together with parsley, freshly ground black pepper to taste, and some of the celery, carrot, and onion from the pot. Add the mustard, and a cup or so of the liquid from the pot. Blend until smooth and creamy, adjusting the seasoning, and adding more of the liquid if necessary.

Remove the meat from the liquid, slice thinly and serve on warmed plates. Serve with the chat potatoes, the remaining baby carrots, and lashings of the sauce. Enjoy!

Note: Dark brown sugar may be substituted for the palm sugar, if necessary.

Graham Shields, Hamilton Island, QLD

SEASONED POCKET STEAK WITH PROSCIUTTO AND NUTS

Serves 4

Every six weeks we have a dinner party with two other couples. We take it in turns and have to put on a four course meal. It has to be like you are going out to a fancy restaurant, but not having to have to pay for it or do the dishes!

I have also done this recipe with chicken breast fillets and it was very nice.

INGREDIENTS

4 pieces of fillet steak
½ red onion, finely diced
40 g prosciutto, finely diced
30 g bacon, diced and cooked
150 g English spinach, steamed then chopped
¼ cup (35 g) crushed pistachio nuts
¼ cup (40 g) pine nuts
½ cup (90 g) diced sun dried tomatoes
½ cup (30 g) fresh breadcrumbs
sea salt and freshly ground pepper
garlic flavoured spreadable feta
spray olive oil
¾ cup (185 ml) dry white wine
1 tablespoon Dijon mustard
1 tablespoon brandy

METHOD

Cut a pocket into the side of the steak then gently beat with mallet to flatten slightly. Combine the onion, prosciutto, bacon, spinach, nuts, sun dried tomatoes and breadcrumbs; season with sea salt and freshly ground black pepper. Open the steak pocket and spread some garlic feta, then spoon in the filling. Close and secure with toothpicks.

Lightly spray a non-stick frying pan with oil and cook the meat for a few minutes on each side. Just before it is cooked to your liking, pour in the wine and cover to infuse the wine flavours. Remove the meat from the pan and set aside. Add mustard and brandy to the pan, bring to the boil and cook until reduced and thickened slightly. Serve with mashed potato, steamed asparagus, snow peas and carrots.

Lorna Clarke, Wickham, WA

BEEF STROGANOFF
Serves 4

When I ask my son what he would like for dinner, he often requests Beef Stroganoff. He loves this dish but I always have to cook mashed potato for him and rice for my husband. My son often cooks this recipe himself so I can have the night off.

INGREDIENTS
500 g fillet or rump steak
butter or oil
1 medium onion, sliced
250 g mushrooms, thinly sliced
⅔ cup (165 ml) water
1 beef stock cube
2 tablespoons tomato paste
sea salt and freshly ground pepper
300 ml sour cream
1 teaspoon cornflour
parsley, chopped, to serve

METHOD
Cut the meat into thin strips across the grain. Heat the butter or oil in a frying pan until very hot, and cook the meat quickly in small batches until brown. Remove from the pan. Add more butter or oil if necessary and sauté the onion and mushrooms until tender.

Return the meat to the pan and add the combined water, stock cube and tomato paste. Stir until combined, and season with salt and pepper. Bring to the boil, reduce the heat and simmer, covered, for 5 minutes.

Put the sour cream and cornflour into a bowl and stir until well combined. Gradually add to the meat mixture, stirring until the sauce boils and thickens. Simmer uncovered for 5 minutes.

Serve with rice, mashed potato or fettucine, and sprinkle with chopped parsley if you like.

Mrs Glenys Paschedag, Molendinar, Qld

MUM'S CURRY
Serves 4–6

My dad was born in Bombay, India, and immigrated with his extended family to Tasmania in 1948. He subsequently worked as a milkman delivering milk to Wivenhoe Primary School, where my mum was a teacher. My mum was a fantastic cook.

Obviously, my dad had a love for real hot curries, and when they first met, my mum had only experienced a typical Australian curry which was very, very mild.

This recipe for Mum's curry, although not as hot as my dad had been used to, seemed the perfect compromise. It has become a family favourite.

INGREDIENTS
- 1 tablespoon butter
- 2 onions, diced
- 2 heaped teaspoons hot curry powder
- 1 tablespoon curry paste
- 750 g rump steak, cubed
- 425 g can diced tomatoes
- 1 teaspoon salt
- 2 tablespoons apricot jam or chutney
- 1 tablespoon brown sugar
- 2 x 425 g cans small potatoes

METHOD

Melt the butter in a large saucepan and fry the onions with the curry powder and curry paste. Add the meat and cook until browned. Add the tomatoes, salt, jam or chutney and sugar. Bring to the boil, stirring constantly. Reduce the heat to low and simmer for 1 hour, then add the potatoes and simmer for another hour.

Serve with cooked basmati rice.

Beth Donoghue, Trinity Beach, QLD

GRANDMA DERKSEN'S NASI GORENG
Serves 4–6

In 1952 my husband's father decided to bring his large family to Australia to escape post-war Holland and seek better opportunities. My mother-in-law was pregnant with her twelfth child. Two children had died in Holland, but a family of ten children is hard to feed and clothe, especially back then.

My husband's uncle had already moved to Australia, having been sponsored by the local dentist in the small Western Queensland town of Miles. This helped others of the family to immigrate to Miles, also.

One of the recipes my mother-in-law adapted is an Indonesian dish called Nasi Goreng. It was not easy to buy many ingredients in Miles, so my mother-in-law made her own version which everyone really enjoys. I've made it for almost 40 years and my daughter and daughters-in-law make it.

INGREDIENTS
    1 tablespoon vegetable oil
    1 kg steak, cubed (or 1.5 kg beef mince)
    1 onion, diced
    2–3 bacon rashers, diced
    ½ red capsicum, diced
    250g spaghetti, broken up and cooked
    45 g packet chicken noodle soup

Method

Heat the oil in a deep frying pan and cook the steak in batches until well browned. Set aside. Fry the onion and bacon. Add capsicum and spaghetti, and return the steak to the pan.

Add the chicken noodle soup and stir through. Pour in just enough water to help cook the noodles in the soup. Cook until tender, stirring to scrape the bottom of the pan occasionally.

We serve it with finely sliced cucumber which has been soaked in mixture of vinegar, water and salt to taste. It is very good with a soft fried egg served on top.

Note: You could use stock powder, soy sauce or kecap manis to season the mixture instead of chicken noodle soup, if you like.

Leila Derksen, Toowoomba, QLD

HUNGARIAN PANCAKES
Serves 4

My brother-in-law escaped from Hungary in 1956. He met my sister one day, proposed the next and she accepted him on the third day. He made this pancake meal for her. It was so unlike the lamb chops and three veg she'd been bought up with and 'so exotic and wonderful', she figured she couldn't go wrong marrying him. And she didn't.

INGREDIENTS

Pancakes
2 cups (300 g) plain flour, sifted
pinch salt
2 eggs
oil, to grease
300 ml milk

Filling
110 g butter or margarine
2 medium onions, sliced
500g beef or veal mince
1 dessertspoon paprika
1 teaspoon tomato paste
1 teaspoon salt
pinch ground black pepper
2 dessertspoons sour cream

Sauce
2 cups (500 g) sour cream
1 teaspoon cornflour
400 g can champignons or 400 g fresh button mushrooms, sliced
plain flour

Method

Preheat the oven to 180°C.

To make the pancakes, mix the flour, salt, eggs and milk to a smooth batter. Make thin pancakes, frying both sides lightly in an oiled pan.

To make the filling, heat the butter or margarine in a saucepan and fry the onions. When beginning to brown, add the meat, paprika, tomato paste and seasonings. Add enough water to barely cover the meat. Put a lid on and simmer for about 15 minutes, stirring occasionally (it may need a little more water). When the meat is cooked, take half the mixture from the pan and set aside. Add the sour cream to the pan and stir until it thickens. Fill the pancakes with this mixture, folding in the edges then rolling them up. Place into a casserole dish and heat for about 30 minutes.

To make the sauce, heat the sour cream in a saucepan. Mix the cornflour with a little of the sour cream and add to the pan with the remaining meat mixture. Bring to the boil and add the mushrooms. Pour the sauce over the heated pancakes and serve immediately.

Val O'Doherty, Coramba, NSW

BOBOTIE

Serves 4–6

Six years ago a large church in Cape Town, South Africa, was in the process of establishing a school for street children. They invited me to join them to set up a library in the school.

Church members were extremely hospitable, and keen to expose me to the full range of South African cuisine. After several meals of Bobotie it soon became my favourite, and one elderly lady gave me this recipe before I returned home.

INGREDIENTS

2 dessertspoons olive oil
3 onions, chopped
2 garlic cloves, crushed
1 teaspoon curry powder
1 teaspoon ground turmeric
1 teaspoon garam masala
1 kg beef mince
3 cups (180 g) fresh breadcrumbs
⅓ cup (80 ml) milk
1 cup (125 g) grated carrot
pinch each of salt, mustard powder, paprika and cinnamon
1 teaspoon curry powder, extra
1 teaspoon ground turmeric, extra
1 teaspoon garam masala, extra
1 dessertspoon chutney (or plum sauce)
½ cup (125 ml) white wine
½ cup (125 ml) vinegar
1 dessertspoon apricot jam
6 bay leaves
4 large eggs
1 cup (250 ml) milk, extra
good pinch dried mixed herbs
garlic salt

Method

Preheat the oven to 180°C.

Heat the oil in a large frying pan and cook the onion and garlic until golden brown. Stir in the curry powder, turmeric and garam masala. Add the mince and cook until browned, stirring to combine and to break up any lumps.

Soak the breadcrumbs briefly in the ⅓ cup (80 ml) of milk and stir into the mince, along with the carrot. Add the salt, spices, chutney, wine, vinegar and jam. Mix until well combined. Cook until carrot is soft. Place into a greased casserole dish (normally square), and arrange the bay leaves evenly on top of meat. Beat the eggs and milk well, and pour over the top. Sprinkle with dried herbs and garlic salt.

Bake for about 45 minutes, until the egg mixture is cooked.

Linda Abblitt, Boat Harbour, TAS

KECAP MANIS KANGAROO
Serves 4

I always like to experiment with new foods and am conscious of how food production affects our environment. That's why I was keen to try cooking kangaroo meat, to support production of 'soft footed' animals that cause less damage to our fragile Australian soils. Thankfully, kangaroo meat is now readily available at my local butcher shop. I love this recipe as it's quick to cook, very low in fat and, of course, delicious.

INGREDIENTS
    2 teaspoons vegetable oil
    2 onions, sliced
    2 garlic cloves, crushed
    500 g kangaroo rump, thinly sliced across the grain
    ½ cup (125 ml) kecap manis (sweet soy sauce)
    sea salt and freshly ground pepper

METHOD
Heat the oil in a non-stick frying pan over high heat. Fry the onion and garlic for about 2 minutes. Add the sliced kangaroo rump and stir-fry until the meat is just pink, about another 2–3 minutes. Add the kecap manis, and season with salt and pepper if desired. Turn the heat down to low for a further 1 minute, then serve.

Serve with steamed rice or couscous, and stir fried vegetables.

Note: It is easier to cut the meat thinly when it is partly frozen.

Janice Sangster, Penshurst, NSW

BEACHED KANGAROO
Serves 2

This is my own recipe, and it has great flavours.

INGREDIENTS
2 tablespoons olive oil
2 kangaroo fillets
4 raw king prawns, peeled

Salad
4 finely shaved slices fennel
1 tablespoon finely sliced zucchini
4 segments navel orange
5 mint leaves, torn
5 coriander leaves
2 basil leaves, torn
2 spring onions, sliced
juice of ½ orange
extra virgin olive oil
sea salt and freshly ground pepper
3 tablespoons Greek style yoghurt

METHOD
Heat the olive oil in a frying pan. Add the kangaroo fillets and cook over high heat for about 2 minutes each side. Add the prawns and cook for a few minutes, until they change colour. Transfer the meat and prawns to a plate to rest.

To make the salad, mix the fennel, zucchini, orange segments, herbs and spring onions together. Dress with the orange juice, a splash of extra virgin olive oil and sea salt and pepper to taste. Mix gently.

To serve, place a dollop of yogurt onto serving plates, and spread it around slightly. Place the kangaroo fillets and prawns on top then the salad. Serve with steamed jasmine rice.

Tony Iommazzo, Glenelg North, SA

Venison Thai vegetable curry
Serves 4

This recipe is also very good with beef mince instead of venison.

Ingredients
½ cup (125 ml) vegetable oil

500 g venison mince

2 small eggplants, cut into small pieces

3 teaspoons Thai green curry paste

1 cup (250 ml) coconut milk

1 cup (250 ml) water

4 kaffir lime leaves

1 tablespoon fish sauce

1 tablespoon brown sugar

1 bunch asparagus, cut into short lengths

1 red capsicum, cut into small pieces

Method
Heat 1 tablespoon of the oil in a wok or deep frying pan. Brown the mince then set aside.

Reserve one tablespoon of the oil, and heat the remaining oil in another pan. Fry the eggplant until brown, then drain on paper towel and set aside.

Heat the reserved oil in the wok. Cook the curry paste over low heat, stirring constantly, for about 2 minutes or until fragrant. Stir in the coconut milk and water, lime leaves, fish sauce, brown sugar and the browned mince.

Simmer for five minutes then add the eggplant, asparagus and capsicum. Simmer for ten minutes, or until vegetables are tender. Serve with steamed rice.

Grace Hadfield, Wodonga West, VIC

GOLF PIE

Serves 4–6

Recently, when visiting a city friend after a long absence, I noticed one of Mum's all-time favourite recipes in her folder. The recipe evolved (there are a few variations) when my mum Gwen began playing golf. She would travel from the family farm, Brynog Ulamambri, to Coonabarabran, about 30 km on a mainly dirt road, each Wednesday in the 1960s. My Dad was very impatient when it came to meal times so she prepared this dish almost every Tuesday evening, and it was usually served with cold sliced lamb in a very short time after golf on Wednesday evening, hence the name.

INGREDIENTS

1.5 kg potatoes, peeled, sliced and par boiled
4 hard boiled eggs, sliced
2 tablespoons butter
1 onion, grated
3 tablespoons plain flour
2 cups (500 ml) milk
2 teaspoons chopped parsley
1 cup (125 g) grated cheese
sea salt and freshly ground pepper
½ cup (25 g) crushed cornflakes

METHOD

Preheat the oven to 180°C.

Arrange the potatoes and eggs in an ovenproof dish. Melt the butter in a saucepan and sauté the onion until soft. Add the flour and cook until lightly browned. Gradually add the milk, stirring to make a thick white sauce. Stir in the parsley and half of the cheese, and season with salt and pepper to taste.

Pour the sauce over the top of the potatoes and eggs. Sprinkle with the crushed cornflakes and remaining cheese. Bake for at least half an hour.

Bronwyn Dawson, Coonabarabran, NSW

Tofu loaf with white miso and tahini

Serves 8

One Christmas about 8 years ago I was asked to contribute to Christmas dinner. I made my tofu loaf which has become a staple in our family, and is always invited back the next Christmas. I must confess that most of the meat eaters come back for seconds of the tofu loaf and not the turkey!

I am the fourth generation in my family who is vegetarian, so making vegetarian and vegan food comes naturally. I am passionate about food that nourishes and heals the body and soul. This recipe is vegan-, wheat-, dairy-, and sugar-free.

Ingredients

Loaf

500 g block of firm tofu, crumbled

1 large onion, finely chopped

2 garlic cloves, crushed

1 cup (60 g) fresh breadcrumbs (use wheat-free bread if wheat intolerant)

1 cup (100 g) rolled oats

3 tablespoons tahini

3 tablespoons tamari (wheat free soy sauce)

2 tablespoons mirin

2 teaspoon curry powder (mild)

100 g tomato paste

1 bunch fresh coriander, chopped

1 bunch flat leaf parsley, chopped

2 medium tomatoes, chopped

1 medium zucchini, chopped

Topping
140 g tomato paste
2 tablespoons mirin
3 tablespoons each sesame seeds, sunflower seeds and pepitas

Sauce
3 tablespoons white miso
3 tablespoons tahini
1 tablespoon apple cider vinegar
1 teaspoon grated ginger
2 tablespoons olive oil
¼ cup (60 ml) water
¼ cup (60 ml) lemon juice
1 teaspoon tamari
freshly ground pepper

METHOD

Preheat the oven to 180°C. Lightly oil a 28 cm x 33 cm x 6 cm deep baking dish.

To make the loaf, combine all the ingredients thoroughly in a large bowl. Press into the prepared dish.

To make the topping, combine the tomato paste and mirin and spread over the top of the loaf. Sprinkle with the seeds. Bake for 1 hour. Stand for 10 minutes before cutting.

To make the sauce, put all the ingredients in a blender and blend until smooth. Add pepper to taste. If you would like the sauce warm, just put it into a saucepan and gently heat until the sauce is just warm, do not boil.

Serve the loaf hot with roasted root vegetables with white miso and tahini sauce or cold on fresh bread with cheese and good tomato relish.

Samantha Jennings, Sapphire Beach, NSW

Side Dishes

CHILLI AVOCADO SALSA

Serves 4

The reason this is such a favourite with our family is all the lovely fresh ingredients. Added to that is the ease of preparation. I serve it with lamb chops, though it is also good with corn chips, pita bread, chargrilled meals or any Mexican food.

INGREDIENTS

3 tomatoes, seeded and diced
1 small red onion, finely chopped
1–2 jalapeno chillies, seeded and very finely chopped
⅓ cup flat leaf parsley
1–2 cloves garlic, crushed
3 tablespoons light olive oil
sea salt and freshly ground pepper
1 ripe avocado
2 limes to garnish

METHOD

Mix the tomatoes, onion, chillies, parsley, garlic and oil together in a bowl. Season to taste, cover and refrigerate for 3 hours.

Just before serving, halve the avocado, remove the stone and gently mash the flesh with a fork while still in the skin. Scoop out the mashed avocado and stir into the salsa. Serve with lime wedges.

Mrs Cathryn Johnston, Condingup via Esperance, WA

BEANS AND POTATO
Serves 1 (multiply as required)

This dish is one I watched my Baba (Croatian for grandmother) cook all my life. Originally, the vegies were boiled and always delicious. No one since has seemed able to get it right; the problem being that too much water ruined it if not drained properly. So I foolproofed the recipe by steaming the potatoes and convincing everyone that you have to be very generous with the oil and salt. According to Baba, you cooked it 'til it's cooked', and added enough oil and salt 'til it tasted right' — those instructions I can't modify!

INGREDIENTS
1 small handful of beans (topped and strung if using runner beans)
1 medium potato, peeled and cut into chunks (the older the potato the better)
very generous glug of olive oil (not extra virgin)

METHOD
Slice the beans diagonally into 6cm pieces. Steam the potatoes until almost cooked, and steam the beans until completely cooked. Transfer the beans and potato to bowl and mash gently with either a masher or a fork. Add the olive oil and season with sea salt to taste.

This recipe is for one, so multiply by however many people you are serving. If using 4 potatoes you will probably need at least ½ cup (60 ml) of olive oil and a tablespoon of salt.

In the unlikely case of having leftovers, add canned tuna, olives, sliced red onion and some good red wine vinegar.

Julie Nolan, Attadale, WA

BROCCOLI SALAD

Serves 4–6

The Harrison Ford film, Witness, *prompted my mother and me to spend two Fall (Autumn) seasons in Lancaster County. We were intrigued and fascinated to spend time in Amish communities, small villages with improbable but novel names like Bird-in-Hand, Intercourse and Paradise.*

I coveted the seemingly stress-free lives of the Amish who spurn the frenetic pace of modern times. Their simplistic and practical approach to life pervaded their cooking.

INGREDIENTS

1 large head broccoli (about 600 g), cut into florets
6 bacon rashers, cut into 1 cm pieces
½ cup (125 g) mayonnaise
2 tablespoons caster sugar
1 tablespoon apple cider vinegar
¼ teaspoon pepper
1 medium red onion, finely sliced
¼ cup (40 g) raisins
¾ cup (115 g) toasted pine nuts

METHOD

Briefly steam the broccoli until brilliant green and tender-crisp. Set aside to cool. Sauté the bacon in a frying pan until just crisp. Whisk together the mayonnaise, sugar, vinegar and pepper.

In a large bowl, gently mix the onions, raisins, broccoli and bacon. Pour the dressing over and combine gently. Refrigerate for 3 to 4 hours before serving. Just before serving, sprinkle over the toasted pine nuts.

Lisa Harris, Aspley, QLD

RED CABBAGE SALAD
Serves 6

We moved into our first home just over 5 years ago. Our immediate neighbours were Greek and prided themselves on their vegetable patch. They welcomed us with their latest harvest — 4 red cabbages. Not wanting to let them go to waste I made cabbage dish after cabbage dish. Once I exhausted every recipe book I possessed I began to experiment. The following recipe ended up being my favourite.

The family enjoys this dish when we have a backyard BBQ. The cabbage makes it crunchy, the mint adds a touch of freshness and the sultanas sweeten it just enough so that the kids love it.

INGREDIENTS
¼ red cabbage, finely sliced
2 medium carrots, grated
½ cup (85 g) sultanas
4 tablespoons slivered almonds
4 sprigs of mint, leaves removed and finely sliced

Dressing
juice of ½ lemon
4 tablespoons olive oil
sea salt and freshly ground pepper

METHOD
Place the cabbage and carrot into a salad bowl, and add the sultanas and slivered almond and mint.

To make the dressing, combine the lemon juice and olive oil. Season with sea salt and cracked pepper to taste. Mix thoroughly and toss through the salad.

Martina Zeitler, Elsternwick, VIC

SAVOURY CHEESE PUFFS
Makes 18

This recipe has been in the family for quite some time. It is very easy to make, and I haven't found anybody who doesn't like my cheese puffs.

INGREDIENTS

1 cup (150 g) self-raising flour, sifted
½ teaspoon baking powder
1½ cups (185 g) grated cheese
1 egg
1 cup (250 ml) cold water
sea salt and freshly ground pepper

METHOD

Preheat the oven to 200°C. Grease 18 patty pans.

Combine the flour, baking powder and cheese in a bowl. Whisk the egg into the water and then stir into flour and cheese. Season with salt and pepper. Place dessertspoons of mixture into the patty pans. Bake for 15 minutes. Serve warm with a little butter. Nice with a bowl of soup.

Variation: Add 2 tablespoons chopped fresh herbs to mixture.

Sonia Benesovsky, Nambour, QLD

Granny Bedford's Delicious Dumplings

Serves 6

I have always loved my Granny Bedford's parsley dumplings recipe. I have made it many times over the years, it being a firm favourite since I was a child.

I haven't always followed the recipe to the letter, but have had my own variations. I like to add cheese to the mixture, and sometimes a small amount of whatever type of curry powder I have on hand as it enhances the flavour of the cheese. Although Granny used them principally in stews, my favourite is adding them to a pot of homemade pumpkin soup.

Granny Bedford is no longer on this earth, but her wonderful simple recipe lives on in our family meals.

Ingredients

2 cups (300g) self-raising flour
¼ teaspoon salt
¼ cup chopped parsley
60g butter
1 egg, beaten
½–¾ cup (125–185 ml) milk

Method

Sift the flour and salt into a large bowl. Add the parsley, and rub in the butter. Add the egg to ½ cup (125 ml) of milk. Add to the flour and stir until the mixture is moist enough to hold together. Use more milk if needed, as it depends on the flour. Don't have the mixture too moist.

Drop spoonfuls of mixture into a simmering stew or soup. Cook tightly covered, for 12–15 minutes, until well risen.

Mrs N Bedford, Taree, NSW

THE BEST POTATO SALAD EVER
Serves 4–6

This recipe is a family favourite and a bit of a family secret, too. I might be in trouble for passing this one on! It came from my Italian uncle Roy who was head wine waiter at the old Romano's many years ago, and like the restaurant, he is long gone. I am sure this came from the Romano's chef. The measurements are not exact, so there has to be a lot of tasting as you go along. I am never short of volunteers, and when they are 'not quite sure', you know it is perfect and that they just want another spoonful!

Three generations of our family really love this one. Tubs were always sent back to boarding school with the kids, and the miserable little flats they moved on to. It must be a sort of comfort food, I guess.

INGREDIENTS
5 medium potatoes
1 small red onion, very finely diced
1 handful of mint leaves, very finely chopped
about 1 tablespoon of extra virgin olive oil
1 teaspoon of salt (but maybe more)
about 1 tablespoon of white vinegar

METHOD
Peel and dice the potatoes. Boil or steam until just tender.

Place the potatoes into a mixing bowl and add the onions and mint. Toss gently, taking care not to break up the potatoes.

Add the olive oil and toss to coat all of the potatoes. You may need more or less, depending on the size and type of potatoes. Add the salt and the vinegar a little at a time, tasting as you go. You will probably need more vinegar and salt than you think, but you will know when you have just the right amount. Chill in the fridge before serving.

Midge Gill, Terrigal, NSW

CURRIED SOUR CREAM JACKET POTATOES

Serves 6

This is a simple variation on the old jacket potato.

INGREDIENTS

6 large potatoes (about 250 g each), scrubbed
300 g sour cream
1 teaspoon curry powder
1 tablespoon fruit chutney

METHOD

Preheat the oven to 180C.

Prick the potatoes, and cook in the microwave for about 20 minutes, turning halfway through cooking, until soft. Once cooked, place into the oven for 35–40 minutes, until the skin is crisp.

Combine the sour cream, curry powder and fruit chutney. Either cut the potatoes in half and makes some cuts in the potato flesh, or cut a deep cross in the top of the whole potato and squeeze to open out slightly. Top with the sour cream mixture and serve immediately.

Larissa Dever, Greenslopes, QLD

HEIDI'S PINE NUT AND PUMPKIN COUSCOUS SALAD

Serves 8

Whenever I'm asked to bring a dish to a friend's BBQ, this is the dish I'm asked to bring. I am always asked for the recipe from those who are trying it for the first time. I can't remember when I started making it or what originally inspired me, but it certainly has evolved over the years. It is easy to make, delicious and healthy — what more could you ask for!

I go by taste rather than measure the ingredients (except for the couscous), and substitute sweet potato for the pumpkin, and baby spinach leaves for the rocket when it takes my fancy. I hope you enjoy my salad.

INGREDIENTS

½ medium butternut pumpkin, cut into 2 cm cubes
⅓ cup (50 g) pine nuts
3 tablespoons olive oil
1 red onion, quartered and thinly sliced
2–3 tablespoons curry powder (or to taste)
2 chicken or vegetable stock cubes
2 cups (400 g) couscous
125 g can chick peas, drained (optional)
½ punnet (125g) cherry tomatoes, halved
rocket leaves, roughly chopped
½ cup roughly chopped coriander leaves

METHOD

Steam or bake the pumpkin until tender. Lightly toast the pine nuts in a dry frying pan over medium heat until golden. Set aside to cool.

Heat 2 tablespoons of the oil in a large non-stick frying pan. Sauté the onion for a couple of minutes over medium heat, then add the curry powder and sauté until the onion is cooked. Reduce the heat to low and add the pumpkin. Mix well to coat the pumpkin in the curry mixture. (I don't like the curry powder to dry out and usually add a little more oil if necessary.)

Meanwhile, place the stock cubes and 2 cups (500 ml) of water into a small saucepan. Add a splash of olive oil and bring to the boil, stirring to dissolve the cubes. Remove from the heat and stir in the couscous. Cover tightly and leave for about 5 minutes, then fluff the grains with a fork to separate. Fold the couscous, pine nuts and chick peas into pumpkin mixture until well combined.

Cool slightly before stirring through the tomatoes, rocket and coriander; this ensures that these ingredients remain fresh and don't wilt before serving.

This salad goes well with any barbecued meat or seafood or is even great on its own.

Heidi Gifford, Hamilton East, NSW

CRUNCHY NOODLE AND GREENS SALAD

Serves 4–6

This dish is one of our family favourites, and every time it is served to guests I am asked to write out the recipe for them. The secret to this beautiful salad is the sweet, cooked sauce. Served chilled, it is delicious poured over anything green, from lettuce to blanched broccoli or beans. (I joke that it would probably make lawn clippings taste good.)

Serve as a salad to accompany a BBQ, or alternatively, in individual bowls topped with sliced grilled meat (chicken breast, steak or prawns) for an impressive, quick meal.

The sauce may be made well in advance.

INGREDIENTS

Sauce

½ cup (125ml) olive oil
⅔ cup (130 g) brown sugar
¼ cup (60 ml) apple cider vinegar
1 tablespoon soy sauce

¼ cabbage, shredded
¼ lettuce, shredded
3 spring onions, thinly sliced
1 small red onion, thinly sliced
250 g fresh mushrooms, thinly sliced
150 g snow peas, blanched, cooled and sliced (or snow pea sprouts)
handful of sunflower seeds
handful of pepitas (dried pumpkin seeds)
handful of slivered almonds
100 g packet fried noodles

METHOD

To make the sauce, combine all the ingredients in a saucepan and stir over low heat until sugar dissolves. While stirring, bring gently to the boil, and simmer for about 5 minutes until reduced slightly. Allow to cool.

Combine all the salad ingredients in a large bowl, topping with noodles. Just before serving, stir sauce well, and toss through salad to taste.

Note: I generally double the sauce ingredients when I make it, as it keeps well in a recycled 'squeeze mayo' container in the fridge for several weeks. Just shake well and pour over 'anything green'.

Elizabeth Frankel, Lowbank, SA

SNOW PEA, GREEN APPLE AND ORANGE SALAD
Serves 1–2

I was making morning tea and lunch for my daughter to take to school. Usually I nibble on the leftovers from making her lunch, this time it was green apple, snow peas and orange. I realised the combination tasted very nice, so later I experimented and made a salad for the family dinner that night. The family loved it. You can use a red apple if you like, though I prefer green.

INGREDIENTS
    1 Granny Smith apple
    3 tablespoons lemon juice, plus extra if desired
    10 snow peas
    1 orange
    ⅓ cup mint leaves, finely shredded

METHOD
Cut the apple in half, remove the core, and cut the flesh into thin strips. Put into a shallow dish and sprinkle with lemon juice to prevent the apples from browning.

Meanwhile, blanch the snow peas by placing into a heatproof bowl and covering with boiling water. Stand for 2 minutes, then drain and put them into icy cold water to keep them bright green. Drain again, then cut into fine long strips. Put into a salad bowl.

Peel the orange, removing all the white pith, and cut the flesh into bite size pieces. Place into the bowl with the snow peas. Drain the apple, and mix with the snow peas and orange.

Toss the mint through, and drizzle with extra lemon juice if desired. Great with pork or lamb.

Olga Fenton, East Lindfield, NSW

SuSu's salad
Serves 4

The simplest dishes often become constant favourites, and the following is one of them.

INGREDIENTS
2 large wet season mangoes (use pawpaw in the dry season)
20 raw snow peas
juice of 2 limes
1 large red chilli, very finely sliced
small handful coriander, roughly chopped

METHOD
Slice the cheeks from the mangoes and remove the skin. Halve the cheeks horizontally then cut into long, thin slices. Arrange alternating mango slices and snow peas into a serving dish, all pointing the same way.

Combine the lime juice and chilli, and pour over the salad. Top with coriander and serve at once.

SuSu Mornane, Larrakeyah, NT

SPINACH SALAD
Serves 6

INGREDIENTS
Dressing
3 tablespoons olive oil
3 tablespoons white wine vinegar
2 tablespoons mango chutney
2 teaspoons sweet chilli sauce
1 teaspoon mustard

150 g packet baby spinach leaves
1 bunch spring onions
1 cup (160 g) raisins
1 green apple, chopped
½ cup (70 g) unsalted mixed nuts
100 g sun dried tomatoes
1 tablespoon sesame seeds

METHOD
To make the dressing, whisk all the ingredients together in a jug, or place into a screwtop jar and shake until combined.

Toss the salad ingredients together in a large bowl, and add the dressing just before serving.

Wendy Duff, Forbes, NSW

SWEET FRIED ONIONS
Serves 4

I hope you love my sweet fried onions as much as we do. As a variation, you can add chopped fresh parsley or chopped fresh thyme.

INGREDIENTS
1 tablespoon oil
2 onions, thinly sliced
¼ cup (50 g) brown sugar
¼ cup (60 ml) balsamic vinegar

METHOD
Heat the oil in a frying pan. Cook the onions over medium heat for 15–20 minutes, stirring often, until brown. Stir in the sugar and vinegar. Cook for about 5 minutes until the vinegar reduces and the mixture is thick.

Serve over steak and garlic mash, or gourmet sausages and mash.

Heather Hargreaves, South Woy Woy, NSW

DESSERTS

CHILLED MARAPOSA SOUP
Serves 4–6

I did a French cooking course about 25 years ago. My husband Don said 'Is this dessert?' Reluctant then, he loves it now, and you will too.

INGREDIENTS
1 kg Maraposa plums (red plums), washed
300 ml water
250 g sugar
2 cinnamon sticks
2 teaspoons ground cloves
1 dessertspoon lemon juice
finely grated rind of 1 lemon
2 cups (500 ml) dry white wine or Rosé
sour light cream, to serve

METHOD
Put the plums into a saucepan with the water. Add the sugar, cinnamon sticks, cloves and lemon juice. Bring to the boil, then reduce the heat slightly and simmer, covered, for 25 minutes. Add the grated lemon rind. Set aside to cool, then remove the cinnamon sticks and de-pip the plums. Strain the liquid and reserve.

Purée the plums in a blender, adding enough of the strained liquid to allow the fruit to blend thoroughly. Pour the purée into a large stainless steel basin and stir in the wine. Put into the fridge to chill. Serve with a good dab of sour light cream.

Shirley Bertram, North Buderim, QLD

BUNDY CHOC BANANAS
Serves 1 (multiply as required)

Recently we were invited to a campfire BBQ in a friend's Bundaberg vineyard and I offered to bring the dessert. I remembered back to my days as a Brownie in Canberra and the campfire cooking. Of course there was no rum in those packages! At the vineyard campfire there was a man from South Africa who had tasted delights in many foreign countries, but exclaimed that this dessert would have to be up there with the best.

INGREDIENTS
1 Cavendish banana, unpeeled
A few squares of dark chocolate
A few raisins marinated in rum (optional)

METHOD
Slit open the banana along the length of the inside curve, but not all the way through. Stuff this cavity with pieces of chocolate and some raisins. Wrap securely in a piece of foil and twist the ends.

Place in the coals of a fire, on the BBQ grill, or bake in the oven for about 15 minutes. To serve, do not unwrap, just slit the package through the foil along the original slit line, then eat with a spoon, scraping out the delicious hot banana and melted chocolate mix. The bananas can be prepared at least 4 hours in advance.

Wendy Fisher, Bundaberg, QLD

FROZEN MANGO MOUSSE

Serves 8

This is a modification of a coffee mousse recipe which was a favourite of my mother's. We adapted it when we moved to Queensland. We made this about 8 years ago for Christmas and it has been on every Christmas table since. Variations have been tried, with coffee and chocolate being popular, as well as rum and raisin. A touch of some liqueur or spirit adds to each. As the mango has such a crisp fresh flavour, it is the current favourite in our home.

INGREDIENTS

6 egg whites
1 cup (220 g) raw sugar
600 ml cream
4–6 mangoes, pureed
1 tablespoon vanilla essence
2 tablespoons brandy

METHOD

Beat the egg whites until stiff then beat in ½ the sugar to make a meringue mixture. In a separate container whip the cream, fold in the mango and add the rest of the sugar a little at a time (stop when it is as sweet you like it). Add the vanilla essence and brandy and beat in. Fold in the meringue mixture, transfer to a clean dish and freeze.

It is easiest to serve if it has been out of the freezer for about 15 minutes.

Nick Woolfield, Wamuran, QLD

PASSIONFRUIT FLUMMERY

Serves 6

During the 1950s I attended the local Catholic primary school. Once a week we rode the rail motor from Edmonton to Gordonvale, to what we called rural school. Here we learnt sewing and cooking. The first garment we made was a skirt when my waist was 24 inches! I still have my recipe book — all neatly hand written with pictures from the Women's Weekly.

INGREDIENTS

1 tablespoon powdered gelatine
½ cup (125 ml) cold water
2 tablespoons flour
½ cup (110 g) sugar
½ cup (125 ml) orange juice
1 tablespoon lemon juice
1 cup (250 ml) hot water
4–6 passionfruit, halved and pulp removed
whipped cream and passionfruit pulp to decorate

METHOD

Sprinkle the gelatine over the cold water. Combine the flour and sugar in a saucepan. Add enough of the orange juice to blend to a smooth paste. Add the remaining orange juice, the lemon juice and hot water. Bring to the boil, stirring until the mixture thickens.

Add the soaked gelatine, stir until dissolved. Cool, then transfer to a large bowl and chill until starting to set.

Using electric beaters, beat well until very thick and pale and at least double in volume. Add the passionfruit pulp and beat well again. Turn into serving dishes and chill until set.

Decorate with lightly whipped cream and extra passionfruit pulp if desired.

Camie McMahon, Edmonton, QLD

ALL-IN-ONE PAVLOVA WITH CARAMEL TOPPING

Serves 6–8

INGREDIENTS

2 egg whites
1 cup (220 g) white sugar
1 teaspoon brown vinegar
4 tablespoons boiling water
pinch salt
1 teaspoon vanilla essence
1 dessertspoon cornflour

Caramel topping
2 egg yolks
25 g butter
½ cup (125 ml) milk
½ cup (100 g) brown sugar
1 tablespoon plain flour
1 teaspoon vanilla essence

whipped cream, to serve

METHOD

Preheat the oven to 150°C. Line a baking tray with foil.

Place the egg whites, sugar, vinegar, water, salt, vanilla essence and cornflour into a large bowl and beat until the mixture is really stiff.

Pile mixture onto the foil in a circle about 22 cm in diameter, and smooth the top slightly. Bake for 30 minutes, then turn the oven off and leave in for another hour. Set aside to cool completely.

To make the caramel topping, mix all the ingredients together thoroughly in a microwave safe bowl. Cook in the microwave on high until thickened, stirring after each minute.

Spread onto the pavlova, then top with whipped cream and topping of your choice.

Mrs Joyce Knobloch, Old Bar, NSW

GINGER BANANA CHEESECAKE
Serves 8–10

INGREDIENTS
    250 g plain sweet biscuits
    125 g butter, melted
    3 tablespoons finely chopped crystallised ginger
    2 teaspoons powdered gelatine
    2 tablespoons hot water
    375 g softened cream cheese
    ½ cup (125 ml) sweetened condensed milk
    ½ cup (125 ml) lemon juice
    2 egg yolks
    1 cup (300 g) mashed bananas (about 3)
    1 cup (250 ml) cream, whipped
    whipped cream, bananas and ginger for garnish

METHOD
Crush the biscuits in a food processor. Combine the biscuit crumbs, butter and ginger in a bowl. Press evenly into a 23 cm spring form tin to form a crust. Chill well. Dissolve the gelatine in hot water. Blend the cream cheese, condensed milk, lemon juice and egg yolks together. Fold in the gelatine, bananas and whipped cream. Spoon into the chilled crumb crust and refrigerate for several hours. Decorate with whipped cream and slices of banana and ginger.

Note: Use well-drained apricots, peaches or mango pulp in place of bananas for a change in flavour.

Mrs Wilma Winter, Lawnton, QLD

ZABAGLIONE
Serves 1 (multiply as required)

My mother, Mary Meoli, had quite a reputation in the Cairns district as a great hostess and provider of spectacular meals with seemingly little effort. Mary would think nothing of making 20 dozen or more meat ravioli, or trays of gnocchi, and she always kept a long cardboard box lined with a seersucker tablecloth full of home-made dried pasta. One of her specialty sweets was Zabaglione. It was the one recipe she taught me well.

INGREDIENTS
2 egg yolks
2 tablespoons caster sugar
2 tablespoons medium sherry or Marsala

METHOD
Using electric beaters, beat the egg yolks on high speed until frothy. Add the caster sugar in two batches and keep beating. After each tablespoon of sugar add one tablespoon of the sherry.

Transfer the well beaten mixture to a double boiler and stir continuously with a wooden spoon for about 10 minutes. The mixture will thicken slightly and become deeper in colour. It should fall off the spoon when tapped on the edge of the saucepan. (Be careful not to have the double boiler touching the water in the bottom or the mixture could curdle.)

Pour into serving dishes and serve with a wafer biscuit. It is best served at room temperature soon after being made.

Note: For a special occasion, fold some thickened cream through the zabaglione, and serve in a hollowed out sponge cake with the top reserved as a lid. Cover with whipped cream and grated chocolate. Refrigerate before serving.

Camie McMahon, Edmonton, QLD

ICE-CREAM PUDDING
Serves 10–12

This recipe is one of my mother's, and has been used on many occasions as I come from a large family (I am one of seven). It was always a favourite for us kids on special occasions. Over the years the family has grown to include many grandchildren for whom this has become a favourite dish, especially requested on birthdays.

As I now live in Darwin it has become a favourite with family and friends at Christmas. It is refreshing in the heat, can be prepared beforehand and does not require cooking, giving more time to relax and enjoy company.

INGREDIENTS
- 1 tablespoon cocoa powder
- 2 tablespoons hot water
- 375 g packet mixed dried fruit
- 2 teaspoons mixed spice
- 1 teaspoon ground cinnamon
- 1 teaspoon ground nutmeg
- 3 tablespoons brandy, rum or sherry
- 600 ml cream
- ⅔ cup (150 g) caster sugar
- 6 egg whites

METHOD
Dissolve the cocoa powder in the hot water. Mix with the fruit, spices and alcohol; leave to stand overnight if possible. Beat the cream and half the sugar, and blend into the fruit mixture.

Beat the egg whites until stiff, and gradually beat in the remaining sugar. Fold gently into the fruit and cream mixture.

Place into a 10-cup capacity bowl lined with foil. Freeze until solid. Turn out onto a cold plate, remove the foil and enjoy!

Wayne Dillon, Darwin, NT

HOT FRUIT COMPOTE
Serves 4

In the late 1970s Mum acquired an electric crockpot. This wonderful appliance allowed food to be cooked slowly and safely for hours, ensuring tenderness, flavour and nutritional benefits. The attractive pottery insert could be put directly onto the table for serving, thus reducing the amount of washing up for the exhausted cook!

Mum tried many dishes in the crockpot, but her favourite was this Hot Fruit Compote. This was a regular dessert and she never varied the recipe, using only the best quality Australian dried fruit.

As well as experiencing a real taste treat, the eater was unlikely to suffer from constipation for the next few days at least!

INGREDIENTS

1 cup (220 g) pitted prunes
1 cup (180 g) dried apricots
225 g can pineapple chunks, undrained
2 cups (500 ml) water

METHOD

Put all the ingredients into the crock pot. Cook covered on low for 7–8 hours, or on high for 3–4 hours.

Serve warm with sour cream and a sprinkling of cinnamon or nutmeg.

Note: This would also make an excellent breakfast dish, served with yoghurt.

Jim Roberts, NSW

Brandied caramel apples
Serves 4

Ingredients
4 green apples, peeled
60 g butter
½ cup (100 g) brown sugar
2 tablespoons brandy
½ teaspoon ground cinnamon
pinch ground nutmeg
pinch mixed spice
cream, to serve

Method
Cut the apples into quarters. Remove the cores and cut into slices. Melt the butter in a frying pan. Add the sugar, stir until combined. Add the apples and stir until coated with the caramel. Add the remaining ingredients and bring to the boil. Boil for 3 minutes. Serve with cream.

Jill Frecklington, Warilla, NSW

FIVE-HOUR NECTARINES IN GINGER SYRUP

Serves 4

I wandered the supermarket one afternoon trying to think of a dessert to cook for friends that night. All I could find was rock-hard, inedible nectarines. I bought a bag of them, determined to turn them into something tasty. The rest was just imagination. Sure enough, slow cooking was very effective and the ginger and vanilla flavours combined perfectly with the sweetness of the nectarines. The double cream is naughty, but worth it.

INGREDIENTS

6 cups (1.5 L) water
3 heaped tablespoons sugar
small knob fresh ginger, peeled and chopped
1 vanilla bean, scored
8–10 new season hard nectarines

METHOD

Combine the water, sugar, ginger and vanilla bean in a large saucepan. Stir to dissolve the sugar then bring to the boil. Reduce the heat slightly and simmer for about 1 hour, until reduced to a thin syrup. Add more water or sugar to taste.

Preheat the oven to low (about 120–150°C).

Cut each nectarine in half and remove the stone carefully so as not to tear away any flesh. Place the nectarine halves in a baking tray with the cut side up. Pour a little of the syrup into each nectarine cup and the remaining syrup, including the ginger chunks, into the baking tray. Save the vanilla bean for later use.

Bake the nectarines for four and a half hours, then turn over and cook for about half an hour more.

Serve with double cream and a little syrup from the baking tray.

Martin Bass, Canterbury, NSW

APPLE PUDDING IN RHYME
Serves 4

As a young West Australian bride of 18 years in 1888, my maternal grandmother was delighted with the wedding gift from her mother. It was a recipe book with one of the family's favourite dessert recipes hand written on the front page.

My mother was thrilled to have a similar recipe book with this same recipe written for her on the front page, in her mother's handwriting, when she and my Dad were married in Sydney in 1926. Carrying on this tradition, my mother did the same thing for me when I married, also in Sydney, at age 18, in 1946.

Here then, still in use and enjoyed in my household, is that same simple recipe, 117 years after my great grandmother first gave it. I have 8 great grandchildren now, so this recipe has been in use for 7 generations that I know of.

INGREDIENTS

Melt in a saucepan with due care,
A tablespoon of butter, fair.
Stir it up till smooth it be.
2 oz flour, stir constantly.
2 cups of milk to it you add,
three minutes boil or you'll be sad.
Next turn into a basin clean
And mix therein with mind serene.
One ounce of sugar, nothing more,
Then beat two yolks and spread them o'er.
The two whites beat to a stiff froth,
To stir together don't be loth
Pour all upon a sweetened bed
Of apples cooked and even spread.
Inside a baking dish then bake.
Just twenty minutes it should take.

Mrs Heather Hastings, Newstead, TAS

BREAD AND BUTTER PUDDING
Serves 6–8

I thought I would tell you one of my favourite desserts, very little changed from the way my mother used to make it.

INGREDIENTS
⅓ cup (55 g) raisins
⅓ cup (60 g) sultanas
rum or brandy
400 ml milk
100 ml thick cream
3 eggs
⅓ cup (75 g) caster sugar
½ teaspoon vanilla essence
¼ teaspoon ground nutmeg
¼ teaspoon ground cinnamon
butter
12 or so slices of 2 or 3 day old white bread, crusts removed
good marmalade with lots of shreds (not too jellified)

METHOD

Marinate the fruit in some rum or brandy, preferably overnight.

Preheat the oven to 180°C.

Whisk together the milk, cream, eggs, sugar, vanilla, nutmeg and cinnamon.

Lightly butter the bread, and put 1 layer in the bottom of a greased shallow casserole dish. Sprinkle with ⅓ of the fruit. Repeat the layers, finishing with bread on top.

Pour the milk mixture slowly and evenly over. Let it soak in, then spread the marmalade evenly over the top. Cover the casserole, and bake for about 30–35 minutes.

Remove from the oven, spread with a little more marmalade if necessary, then caramelise (even burn slightly), with a brulée burner, or under a hot grill.

Serve with custard or cream.

Note: You can use raisin or fruit bread, in which case reduce the quantity of fruit, and omit the nutmeg and cinnamon. Add or substitute other fruits, such as blueberries or pitted black cherries.

Graham Shields, Hamilton Island, QLD

NANA'S SELF-SAUCING CHOCOLATE PUDDING

Serves 6

This is Nana's Chocolate Pudding which we all just love. In fact, we love everything that Nana makes, but her choccie pudding is pretty special.

What makes the recipe special is that she doesn't know where it came from but it lives in her very precious 'black book', where everything important is — our dental records as we grew up, our shoe sizes as we grew up, all the family birthdays and all her recipes.

I particularly like that she carries the recipe now in her toiletry bag so that she can produce it on request when she is away from home. She is regularly asked to make that pudding.

I did suspect strongly that what makes it extra special for us is that she makes it, and as one of her grandkids said, 'everything tastes better at Nan's'.

INGREDIENTS

1 cup (150 g) self-raising flour
½ teaspoon salt
¾ cup (165 g) sugar
2 tablespoons cocoa powder
½ cup (125 ml) milk
1 teaspoon vanilla essence
2 tablespoons butter, melted
2 tablespoons chopped nuts (optional)
¾ cup (185 ml) brown sugar
½ cup (60 g) cocoa powder, extra
1½ cups (375 ml) boiling water

Method

Preheat the oven to 180°C. Grease a 6-cup capacity casserole dish.

Sift together all the dry ingredients, and add the milk, vanilla essence, butter and nuts if using. Stir until smooth, and place into the prepared dish.

Mix the brown sugar, cocoa powder and boiling water together and pour over the uncooked pudding. Bake for 40 minutes or until it looks like it's cooked.

Colleen Kavanagh, Moonee Ponds, VIC

CARAMEL NUT SELF-SAUCING PUDDING

Serves 4–6

I was only 16 years old when my mother died, and many of the memories we have of her seem to involve all the wonderful food she made. Before I left home I made sure I salvaged her handwritten recipes that she kept in a stained and well-used exercise book. I found all sorts of fantastic recipes, but this seems to be one that we all agreed we loved the most. Even now when I make it for my children, there is something comforting in its warm gooiness that brings me back to it time and time again.

INGREDIENTS

¾ cup (115 g) self-raising flour
¼ cup (30 g) ground hazelnuts
400 ml condensed milk
1 tablespoon butter
1 teaspoon vanilla essence
⅓ cup (80 ml) milk
1 cup (200 g) firmly packed brown sugar
1¾ cups (440 ml) boiling water

METHOD

Preheat the oven to 180°C. Grease a 6-cup capacity baking dish.

Sift the flour into a bowl and stir in the hazelnuts. Place the condensed milk in saucepan and stir over moderate heat for 10 minutes or until thickened and slightly golden brown. Add the butter, vanilla essence and milk, and stir until the butter melts. Let cool slightly.

Pour the milk mixture into the dry ingredients and mix well. Pour the batter into the prepared dish. Sprinkle brown sugar over the top of the pudding. Carefully pour boiling water evenly over the top of the pudding. Bake in oven for about 35 minutes or until firm. Let stand for 5 minutes before serving.

Mesha Hall, Wagin, WA

STICKY DATE PUDDING
Serves 6–8

We lived on a cream dairy farm, not financially abundant, but with ample milk, cream, butter, eggs, poultry and homegrown vegies. We'd catch a duck and give it to Mum to cook. The duck and vegies would go into the oven (an old silver and green cast iron wood stove) after the magnificent sticky date pudding came out. Sunday wasn't Sunday without it.

INGREDIENTS

200 g dates, pitted
1 cup (250 ml) water
1 teaspoon bicarbonate of soda
100 g butter
⅔ cup (150 g) caster sugar
2 large eggs, beaten
1½ cups (225 g) self-raising flour, sifted

Caramel sauce
1 cup (200 g) brown sugar
1½ cups (375 ml) cream
100 g butter

METHOD

Preheat the oven to 160°C. Grease a 20 cm round cake tin.

Combine the dates and water in a saucepan and bring to the boil. Remove from the heat and stir in the bicarb. Cool. Beat the butter and sugar, and add the eggs. Fold in the flour and date mixture. Spread into the tin, and bake for 45 minutes.

To make the sauce, combine all the ingredients in a saucepan. Bring to the boil. Simmer for 2 minutes. Pour over the pudding and serve with custard.

Deborah Dimmick, Noosaville, QLD

LEMON SPONGE PUDDING

Serves 3–4

My recipes have been in my possession for more than fifty years. I learned to cook using Our Church Recipe Book *(Highfields Methodist) and the Lemon Pudding was in this. My grandchildren enjoy these recipes too, so they have stood the test of time.*

INGREDIENTS

1 tablespoon butter
¾ cup (165 g) sugar
1 egg, separated
juice of 1 lemon
2 tablespoons self-raising flour
1 cup (250 ml) milk

METHOD

Preheat the oven to 170°C. Grease a 4-cup capacity ovenproof dish.

Cream the butter and sugar, then beat in the egg yolk and lemon juice. Fold in the flour and milk. Beat the egg white until stiff, and fold into the mixture.

Pour into the prepared dish. Place into a baking tin and fill with enough water to come halfway up the side of the pudding dish. Bake for 35–45 minutes, until set. The sauce is on the bottom, sponge on top. Yummy!

Serve cold or warm, with cream or ice-cream.

Note: This recipe may be doubled to serve more people.

Irene Brock, Raymond Terrace, NSW

NANNA'S DELICIOUS STEAMED PUDDING

Serves 6

This recipe originated in the 1940s, when making a living was tougher than today. My very precious and much loved grandmother, who was the adored mother of her 10 children and lived to be 98 years of age, gave me this 'Delicious Home-Made Steamed Pudding' recipe when I was 14. I'm now 52 years old. It's always been a huge favourite of mine, my children, family and friends for many years.

I've written this recipe out for others to try almost more times than I've blinked my eyes in the time of cooking it.

INGREDIENTS

1 tablespoon butter or margarine, melted

1 tablespoon brown or white sugar

pinch salt

½ cup (160 g) raspberry jam (can use any jam, but I always prefer raspberry)

few drops lemon essence

½ cup (125 ml) tea (make tea in pot as usual, let stand a while)

½ cup (30 g) fresh breadcrumbs

1 cup (185 g) mixed dried fruit

1 cup (150 g) and 2 dessertspoons self-raising flour

METHOD

Mix all the ingredients together. Place into a greased 4-cup capacity pudding basin. Cover with a sheet of baking paper and foil. Tie a string around the paper and foil to secure, and place into a large pot. Half fill with boiling water, cover and steam for 2–2½ hours, until cooked when tested with a skewer.

Delicious hot or cold with custard, cream or ice-cream, or with all three.

Jennifer Singh, Drouin, VIC

PUDDING
Serves 8

A handy recipe for a pudding either served hot with custard, or as a tasty morning tea treat. In winter, the aroma of this recipe means home to me.

INGREDIENTS
375 g mixed fruit
250 g chopped dates
1 cup (250 ml) water
1 cup (200 g) brown sugar
1 cup (250 ml) strong honey
½ teaspoon bicarbonate of soda
1 teaspoon ground nutmeg
1 teaspoon ground cinnamon
½ cup (45 g) desiccated coconut
2½ cups (375 g) self-raising flour, sifted
2 eggs, lightly beaten
slivered almonds, to decorate

METHOD
Preheat the oven to 180°C. Grease an ovenproof dish approximately 30 cm x 23 cm x 6 cm.

Combine the mixed fruit, dates, water, sugar and honey in a saucepan. Bring to the boil, then reduce the heat and simmer until the butter has melted and fruit is soft. Remove from heat, and stir in the bicarb, nutmeg, cinnamon and coconut. Set aside to cool.

When the mixture is cool, fold in the flour and eggs. If you think the mixture is too thick, orange juice or a bit of milk can be added. Spoon into the prepared dish and level the surface. Sprinkle over the slivered almonds. Cook for 40–45, until cooked when tested with a skewer.

Relma Lardner, South Maroubra, NSW

Joanne's (Mum's) custard
Serves 4–8 (depending on serving style)

This custard is delicious. Mum got the recipe from her friend Robyn when I was growing up. When I left home, it was one of the first recipes I asked her for! Once you have tasted this, you will never buy custard from the shop ever again! Fussy adults through to babies starting on solids love this. It can be served with a pudding, in a flan, in cream puffs or simply in a ramekin, in much the same way as you would have Crème Caramel. It is so easy and just divine.

Ingredients
800 ml milk (I use full cream, but any would be fine)
2 tablespoons plain flour
1 teaspoon cornflour
½ cup (110 g) sugar
1 egg
1 tablespoon butter
1 teaspoon butter (extra)

Method
Slowly heat the milk in a double boiler, or in a bowl over a saucepan of hot water. It really is better to not have direct heat, but if you don't have a double boiler, it will still work — you'll just have to stir faster and watch it closely!

Mix the flours, sugar, egg and butter in a large coffee mug or small bowl, so it becomes like a thick paste.

Add 2–3 tablespoons of the warm milk and stir into the paste. Add more milk to the paste and stir. Continue doing this until the paste mixture is very runny (and warm), say, three or four times. The runnier the paste is, the better it will blend with the remaining milk on the stove.

Add the runny paste mixture to the remaining milk on the stove, and bring the water in the double boiler to the boil. The custard will start to thicken. You can remove the pot from the heat, if you think it's thickening faster than you can stir. Stir with a wooden spoon, or better still, use a whisk. It will thicken quickly and you want to avoid lumps.

If you get lumps, don't lose hope, whisk furiously, or beat with an egg beater — it will still be wonderful, believe me!

Once thickened, add the extra teaspoon of butter and stir in.

Serve as desired. Immediately is my preference, but it also sets very well and keeps well in the fridge covered with plastic wrap or in an airtight container. Best used within 24 hours.

Rachel Morse, Leura, NSW

HOT LOGANBERRY TRIFLE
Serves 8

This is an old favourite. It is delicious and never fails to get requests for seconds.

INGREDIENTS
1 jam-filled Swiss roll, sliced
¼ cup (80 g) plum or strawberry jam
⅓ cup (40 g) custard powder
1 tablespoon honey
1 tablespoon sugar
3 eggs, separated
2 tablespoons milk
2 cups (500 ml) milk, extra
2 x 410 g cans loganberries or boysenberries, drained
½ cup (110 g) caster sugar

METHOD
Preheat the oven to 160°C. Grease an 8-cup capacity casserole dish.

Arrange the Swiss roll slices over the base and sides of the prepared dish. Spread the jam over.

Mix together the custard powder, honey, sugar, egg yolks and the 2 tablespoons of milk until smooth.

Heat the extra milk in a heavy-based saucepan until boiling. Lower the heat and gradually stir in the custard mixture until it boils and thickens (about 3 minutes). Remove from the heat. Spoon the berries over the cake then pour the custard over.

In a separate bowl, beat the egg whites until stiff. Add the caster sugar and beat well for about 4 minutes, until thick and glossy. Pile the meringue onto the pudding. Bake for about 10 minutes, or until lightly browned.

Mollie Bye, Bothwell, TAS

NECTARINE, GINGER & ALMOND DESSERT CAKE WITH BERRY COULIS

Serves 6–8

I invented this recipe because of seasonal nectarine excesses, when we beat the birds to eating our fruit! After nectarine season, I substitute pears for the nectarines, then later on I use quinces and call it Quince Charming Cake!

INGREDIENTS

200 g nectarines, approximately
125 g butter
120 g brown sugar
2 eggs
½ teaspoon ground ginger
20 g ground almonds
1 cup (150 g) self-raising flour, sifted
90 ml milk
30 g slivered almonds
50 g crystallised ginger, finely chopped

Syrup
1½ tablespoons sugar
⅓ cup (80 ml) water

Berry coulis
750 g raspberries
½ cup (110 g) caster sugar
1 tablespoon lemon juice
1 tablespoon brandy or liqueur (optional)

METHOD

Preheat the oven to 160°C. Grease a 20 cm cake tin and line the base with baking paper.

Slice the nectarines thinly. Cream the butter and brown sugar in food processor. Whizz in the eggs, ginger and almonds. Mix in the flour and milk alternating ⅓ at a time. Briefly, whizz in half the silvered almonds. (If the mixture seems dry add a little more milk, but don't make it too soft or the nectarines fall to the bottom). Place ⅞ of the cake mixture into the tin.

Sprinkle chopped ginger over the top of cake mixture. Arrange the nectarine slices in a circular fashion around the cake, ensuring that the nectarine skins are covered by cake mix. Thinly spread the remaining cake mixture over the top, and sprinkle with the remaining slivered almonds. Bake for about 50 minutes, until a skewer inserted into the centre comes out clean. Stand the cake in the tin while making the syrup.

To make the syrup, combine the sugar and water in a small saucepan. Stir over low heat to dissolve the sugar, then bring to the boil and simmer for about 5 minutes, until syrupy.

Turn the cake out on to a wire rack, then invert onto a serving plate. Brush the top and sides of the warm cake with the syrup. Cover the cake with plastic wrap to keep the moisture in as it cools.

To make the berry coulis, whizz all the ingredients in a food processor until the sugar is dissolved. Push through a coarse sieve to remove the berry seeds. Check flavour for sweetness and add a little more sugar if necessary.

Serve coulis over the warm cake and offer cream or ice-cream.

Annette Mouat, Mandurang, VIC

TOFFEE FIG AND CHOCOLATE TART

Serves 8

This idea came to me one night when my sister asked me to make a dessert for a dinner party. It's great because you actually get two desserts (the tart and half a chocolate cake). Watch the syrup though. When I first made it I left the figs for too long, forming a wonderful fig and orange toffee, but the cake didn't absorb it so it set on top. Still nice, but not the desired outcome!

INGREDIENTS

Shortcrust pastry
1¼ cups (185 g) plain flour
1 tablespoon caster sugar
90 g cold butter, cut into pieces
1 egg yolk
1–2 tablespoons chilled water
100 g good quality dark chocolate (min 70% cocoa solids), melted

Chocolate filling
250 g unsalted butter, softened
1 cup (220 g) caster sugar
3 eggs, lightly beaten
½ cup (125 ml) milk
1 teaspoon vanilla extract
70 g ground almonds
4 tablespoons dark cocoa powder, sifted
1 cup (150 g) self-raising flour, sifted

For the toffee figs
300 g (about 15) dried figs
1 cup (250 ml) orange juice
1 cup (250 ml) water
2 cups (440 g) sugar

Method

To make the shortcrust pastry, put the flour, sugar and butter into a food processor and pulse until the mixture resembles breadcrumbs. Add the egg yolk and sufficient water for mixture to come together into dough. Form a ball, wrap in plastic wrap and refrigerate for 15 minutes. Roll out as thinly as possible (between two sheets of plastic wrap or on a lightly floured surface), and place gently into a 30 cm flan tin. Return to fridge for 30 minutes.

Preheat the oven to 200°C. Prick the base of the pastry with a fork and line with crumpled baking paper. Fill with pastry weights, uncooked rice or beans. Cook for 15 minutes or until the pastry looks dry, but not fully cooked. Remove the weights and cook for another 5 minutes or until golden. Allow to cool in the tin on a wire rack. Once cool, spread the melted chocolate over the base and sides of the pastry case. Refrigerate until needed.

Preheat oven to 180°C. Grease and line a 23 cm springform tin.

To make the chocolate filling, which is in fact a chocolate cake, beat the butter and sugar in a large bowl. Add the eggs, milk and vanilla and beat until combined. Fold in the ground almond, cocoa and flour, until smooth. Pour into the cake tin and bake for 45–50 minutes or until springy when pressed.

To prepare the figs, make a cut in the bottom of each fig. Tear them open and flatten them out, making their surface area as large as possible. Combine the orange juice, water and sugar in a saucepan, and stir over a low heat to dissolve the sugar. Add the figs, increase the heat and boil for 10 minutes. Do not allow the syrup to reduce too much, it must be thin enough to absorb into the chocolate filling. Remove from the heat and use a fork or a slotted spoon to remove the figs. Place onto a wire rack to cool. Reserve the syrup.

To assemble the tart, cut half the chocolate cake into slices (reserve the rest for another use) and crumble into the tart shell. Spoon half the syrup over the cake. Arrange the figs on top and pour the other half of the syrup over the tart.

Fiona Scarlett, Traralgon, VIC

PLUM TART
Serves 6

INGREDIENTS
1 large sheet frozen shortcrust pastry, thawed
2 cups of blood-red plums
2–3 tablespoons sugar
2 eggs
½ teaspoon ground star anise
½ cup (125 ml) milk, approx.
bit of rum or something similar
icing sugar, to dust

METHOD
Preheat the oven to 160°C. Line a 23 cm tart tin with the pastry and trim the edges. Lay a sheet of non-stick baking paper over the pastry and fill with dried beans or rice. Bake for 10 minutes, then remove the paper and beans and cook a further 10 minutes, or until golden. Set aside to cool.

Place the plums and sugar (the amount will vary according to the sweetness of the plums) into a bowl and cook in the microwave, until the plums are soft but before they break down into a pulpy mess. Leave until cool enough to handle, then remove the stones. Place the plums into a food processor with the eggs, star anise and enough milk to purée to the consistency of yoghurt. Add a bit of rum, according to your own preference. Pour the plum mixture into the pastry case, and cook for 35–45 minutes, until set.

Cool and dust with icing sugar. Serve with cream, ice-cream or yoghurt on the side.

Note: You can use any fruit that is ripe, available and that can be cooked and pureed, such as quinces, rhubarb or blackberries. For extra flavour you could use cinnamon, cloves, ginger or nutmeg depending on preference. Instead of rum you can try anything you fancy, or leave it out altogether.

Alan Carlton, Newtown, TAS

MUM'S BAKED APPLE DUMPLINGS
Makes 10

My mum, Gwynny Morley, always made this sweet when my brother Bill came home on leave from the army.

INGREDIENTS

Pastry

125 g butter or margarine
1¼ cups (185 g) plain flour
1¼ cups (185 g) self-raising flour
good pinch salt

Filling

10 granny smith apples, peeled and cored
10 teaspoons sugar
3 tablespoons of golden syrup
1 dessertspoon butter

METHOD

Preheat the oven to 230°C.

To make the pastry, rub together the butter, flour and salt. Mix with enough water (2–3 tablespoons) to make a dough. Divide the dough into 10 portions. Roll out each piece into a round large enough to enclose an apple.

Place an apple on a piece of pastry and sprinkle with a teaspoon of sugar. Cover the apples with the pastry and place into a baking dish. Repeat with the remaining apples and pastry. Drizzle with the golden syrup, then pour in enough boiling water to come halfway up the apples. Place the butter into the dish.

Place into the oven and bake until the pastry starts to brown. Reduce the temperature to 180°C, and baste with the liquid every 15 minutes. After 1 hour the pastry should be crisp and brown on top and syrupy and soft on the bottom. Always serve with homemade custard.

Michael J Roach

GOLDEN SYRUP DUMPLINGS
Serves 4

INGREDIENTS

1 cup (150 g) self-raising flour, sifted
1 tablespoon butter
milk

Syrup
½ cup (110 g) sugar
1 dessertspoon butter
1 cup (250 ml) boiling water
1 tablespoon golden syrup

METHOD

Rub the flour and butter together. Mix in enough milk to make a sticky dough.

To make the syrup, combine the ingredients in a wide saucepan or deep frying pan. Bring to the boil and cook for several minutes. Drop in tablespoons of dough (about 12), cover and simmer for 12 minutes.

Marcia Scholz, Wudinna, SA

PUFTALOONS
Makes about 12

This recipe came from my grandmother-in-law. Gran, of course, never had measurements. When she was living with us, I used to measure each of the ingredients as she prepared 'smoko' for us when we came home from school (both my husband and I were teachers at the time). Our son adored the puftaloons and now prepares them as an Aussie treat for his son, as they live in the USA.

INGREDIENTS
½ cup (75 g) self-raising flour
1 tablespoon sugar
pinch of salt
1 dessertspoon custard powder
1 egg, beaten
¼ cup (60 ml) water (more if too thick)
vegetable oil, to deep fry
golden syrup, to serve

METHOD
Sift together the flour, sugar, salt and custard powder. Add the egg and water.

Half fill a large saucepan with oil and heat. Cook spoonfuls of the mixture in hot oil, turning until puffed and golden.

Serve hot with lots of golden syrup. Yum.

Chris Clarke, Nowra, NSW

Golden walnut topped dessert

Serves about 20

This recipe was given to me by a beautiful Sri Lankan friend and it is always a hit whenever my daughters or I make it. It is easy to make, has such a lovely, unique flavour and it disappears very quickly — a very good sign. It is great to serve at a barbecue or casual luncheon when one has a gathering of family and friends. Everyone asks for the recipe.

Ingredients

¼ cup (60 ml) boiling water
1 cup (125 g) quick oats
⅓ cup (75 g) white sugar
⅓ cup (65 g) brown sugar
60 g butter
1¼ cups (185 g) self-raising flour
1 teaspoon bicarbonate of soda
½ teaspoon ground nutmeg
2 eggs, lightly beaten

Topping
125 g soft butter or margarine
½ teaspoon vanilla essence
¼ cup (60 ml) cream or evaporated milk
1 cup (125 g) walnuts
⅓ cup (75 g) sugar
¼ cup (25 g) desiccated coconut

METHOD

Preheat the oven to 180°C. Grease a 25 cm x 35 cm baking dish.

Pour the water over the oats, sugars and butter. Cover and stand for 20 minutes. Sift the dry ingredients into the mixture, then mix in the eggs. Bake for 35–40 minutes, then cool completely.

To make the topping, mix all the ingredients together. Spread over cooled cake. Place under a grill and cook until golden. Watch carefully as it can burn very quickly.

I make it ahead of time and then pop under the grill just before serving. Cut into squares and serve with whipped cream. Can also be served cold, as a slice.

Note: You could use slivered almonds or sunflower seeds instead of walnuts, if you like.

E Joan Knight, Eagle Point, VIC

GOLDEN STAIRCASE PIE
Serves 6–8

This recipe was given to me by my dear mother-in-law, who recently celebrated her 90th birthday. This dessert is a family favourite and always attracts compliments when served to friends on special occasions.

INGREDIENTS

Pastry
90 g butter
3 tablespoons caster sugar
1 egg yolk
1 tablespoon milk
1¼ cups (185 g) self-raising flour, sifted
3 tablespoons cornflour, sifted

First layer
juice of 2 lemons
pulp of 3 passionfruit
250 ml sweetened condensed milk

Second layer
juice and finely grated rind of 1 lemon
juice and finely grated rind of 1 orange
1 tablespoon custard powder
1 tablespoon cornflour
3 tablespoons sugar
water
1 tablespoon butter

Topping
1 cup (250 ml) thickened cream
2 tablespoons icing sugar
passionfruit pulp, to decorate

Method

Preheat the oven to 180°C.

To make the pastry, cream the butter and sugar together, then beat in the egg yolk. Add the milk, and work in the flour and cornflour. Knead lightly on a floured board until smooth, then roll out and lift carefully into a 21 cm pie plate. Trim and decorate the edge. Prick all over with a fork. Bake for 20 minutes then set aside to cool.

To make the first layer, combine all the ingredients. Spread into the pastry shell and chill.

To make second layer, add water to the lemon and orange juice to make up to 1 cup (250 ml). Place into a saucepan with the grated rinds. Bring to the boil. Blend custard powder, cornflour and sugar with enough water to make a smooth paste. Add the boiling juices slowly, stirring constantly. Add the butter, return to a low heat and stir for 3 minutes. Allow to cool, stirring occasionally to prevent a skin forming. Spread over the first layer and chill.

To make the topping, whip the cream and icing sugar in a small bowl with an electric mixer until soft peaks form. Cover the top of the pie with cream and decorate with passionfruit pulp. Refrigerate until ready to serve.

Gloria Newton, Jindalee, QLD

TEA-TIME TREATS

UNCLE DION'S CHOCOLATE BISCUITS
Makes about 15

I call these 'Uncle Dion's Chocolate Biscuits' because I have made them with my nephews. I came about this recipe after being unsatisfied with other biscuit recipes. There are certain differences in my recipe. I use both plain and self-raising flour because the self-raising flour makes the biscuit rise and gives it a nice cakey texture. The custard powder is something my grandmother used to use. It gives the biscuit a good flavour.

INGREDIENTS
    1 cup (150 g) plain flour
    1 cup (150 g) self-raising flour
    1½ teaspoons baking powder
    ½ teaspoon salt
    ⅓ cup (40 g) custard powder
    ½ cup (60 g) chocolate icing sugar
    125 g butter
    2 eggs
    ½ cup (220 g) caster sugar
    ⅔ cup (170 ml) milk

METHOD
Preheat the oven to 180°C. Grease two oven trays.

Sift the flours, baking powder, salt, custard powder and icing sugar into a bowl. In a separate bowl, beat the butter, eggs and caster sugar with electric beaters until creamy. Then, bit by bit, add the flour mixture. When it resembles a coarse meal, add the milk. If mix is too sloppy, add a little more flour. Roll into balls, place onto prepared trays and flatten slightly. Bake for 15–20 minutes, or until cooked.

Note: Chocolate icing sugar is available in the supermarket where you get the normal icing sugar.

Dion Stewart, North Beach, WA

JAM DROPS

Makes about 30

My darling Grandmother was a country woman who made good plain food and plenty of it. Every morning and afternoon she would take the billy full of hot tea and a plate of homemade goodies to my Grandfather if he was working in the paddocks. Whilst her sponges were not known for their lightness, she made the best jam drops and ginger snaps ever. Her recipe book was a cut-down school exercise book that I have now framed and hung with love on my kitchen wall.

INGREDIENTS

125 g butter
¾ cup (165 g) sugar
2 eggs
vanilla essence
pinch salt
2 cups (300 g) plain flour
2 teaspoon baking powder
⅓ cup (100g) jam of choice

METHOD

Preheat the oven to 190°C. Grease two oven trays.

Cream the butter and sugar. Add the eggs and beat well. Add vanilla and salt to taste. Sift the flour and baking powder over the butter mixture and combine. Roll mixture into small balls and place onto the prepared trays. Use your thumb to make an indentation into each ball and fill with a little jam. Bake for 10–12 minutes, until golden brown. Take care as the jam will be very hot.

Catherine Kembrey, Albury, NSW

GINGERNUTS
Makes about 42

In a dog-eared notebook was a recipe for Gingernuts, which Nanna had made for her family since 1934, when she was married. A close friend had given it to her. Every time we went to visit, she always had a tin of biscuits for us, for when we were 'peckish'.

INGREDIENTS
4 cups (600 g) plain flour, sifted
2 tablespoons ground ginger
2 teaspoons bicarbonate of soda
1½ cups (330 g) sugar
185 g butter, melted
1 cup (250 ml) golden syrup
1 egg

METHOD
Preheat the oven to 180°C. Grease two oven trays.

Mix the flour, ginger and bicarb in a bowl. Add the sugar, butter, golden syrup and egg. Roll into balls, place onto a tray and flatten.

Bake for 12–15 minutes.

Miss Margaret Corfield, Brooweena, QLD

SCOTCH SHORTBREAD

Makes about 30 fingers

In 1960 my father, a TAA airline pilot, was seconded to the RFDS, based in Charters Towers, QLD. At the Oak Park Races, this wonderful Scotch shortbread was offered amongst other marvellous foods. One of the station ladies wrote out the recipe for my mother, then a young wife and new mother. Forty-four years later, the worn recipe for our family favourite is tucked in the front of an equally loved and much used copy of Amy Schauer. It is used frequently throughout the year, and of course at Christmas.

INGREDIENTS

250 g butter
1 cup (125 g) pure icing sugar (not mixture), sifted
2 dessertspoons cornflour
2 cups (300 g) plain flour
pinch of salt

METHOD

Preheat the oven to 180°C. Grease a 23 cm x 30 cm slice tin.

Cream the butter and icing sugar. Sift the cornflour and plain flour together, and gradually add to the butter mixture. Do not overbeat. Gently pat the mixture into the prepared tray.

Bake for 30 minutes. Cool, then slice into fingers or squares, to suit.

Note: The mixture will not change very much in colour during cooking.

Lisa Harris, Aspley, QLD

CRUNCHIES
Makes 24

Growing up as a primary school child in the 1960s, my mother always had biscuit tins filled with delicious treats. However, after several years of the same biscuits and slices, the enjoyment of eating them was waning. Fortunately, my best friend's mother was the Canteen Manager, so she had a huge choice of gigantic, mouth-watering cakes for her lunch each day! As best friends would, we often swapped our treats and I adored devouring a cinnamon scroll or vanilla slice while my friend ate her small home-cooked Crunchie. I always felt I had the better deal, but no doubt so did she!

INGREDIENTS
    125 g margarine or butter
    1 tablespoon golden syrup
    ½ cup (85 g) sultanas (or other dried fruit)
    3 cups (300 g) rolled oats
    ½ cup (110 g) sugar

METHOD
Preheat the oven to 180°C. Grease a 20 cm x 30 cm lamington tin.

Melt the margarine or butter over a gentle heat and add the golden syrup and sultanas. Mix in the dry ingredients. Press into the prepared tin and bake for 15 minutes.

Cut into squares while warm, then cool and store in an airtight container.

Note: You could reduce the oats to 2 cups (220 g), and add 1 cup (90 g) of desiccated coconut, if you like.

Mrs Jane Brotherson, Leeming, WA

CORNFLAKE BISCUITS
Makes about 16

This quick and easy recipe was handed down from Ivy and George Gosling of Blackwood. George never minded going out and chopping the wood to stoke the stove for Ivy to make his favourite biscuits — he only complained there were never enough!

INGREDIENTS
125 g butter or margarine
¾ cup (165 g) sugar
1 egg
1 cup (150 g) self-raising flour, sifted
1 cup (175 g) sultanas
cornflakes, to coat

METHOD
Preheat the oven to 180°C. Grease two baking trays.

Using electric beaters, beat the butter and sugar until light and creamy. Beat in the egg. Fold in the flour and sultanas. Take small spoonfuls of the mixture, make into balls and roll in cornflakes. Place onto the prepared tray and bake for about 30 minutes.

Mrs Frances Dillon, Melton South, VIC and
Mrs Olive Cann, Blackwood, VIC

WIRELESS BISCUITS
Makes about 28

This biscuit recipe has been made in our family as long as I can remember. Mother used to make them, tightly pack them in a tin wrapped in calico and send them to my father serving in New Guinea and the Solomon Islands during the war. He said they never arrived in crumbs! Our children (and theirs) love them, as do friends. Of all the biscuits I make for Christmas giving, these are the top favourite. Must say something about them!

INGREDIENTS
125 g butter
1 tablespoon golden syrup
1 teaspoon bicarbonate of soda
¾ cup caster sugar
2 tablespoons boiling water
¾ cup (45 g) shredded coconut
¾ cup (115 g) plain flour, sifted
1 cup (95 g) flaked oatmeal

METHOD
Preheat the oven to 160°C. Grease two baking trays.

Place the butter, golden syrup, bicarb and sugar into a saucepan with the boiling water. Bring to the boil, then add the other ingredients and mix well. Place heaped teaspoons of mixture onto the prepared tray, allowing room for spreading. Bake for 20–30 minutes. They should be deliciously thin and crisp, but not over browned.

Note: You can do the melting in the microwave instead of a saucepan if you like. Chopped walnuts make a great addition to these biscuits.

Priscilla Nankervis, Brighton East, VIC

DATE AND SWEET POTATO SLICE
Makes about 18

INGREDIENTS
½ cup (125 ml) olive oil
¾ cup (150 g) brown sugar
½ cup (80 g) chopped pitted dates
¼ cup (55 g) chopped glacé pineapple (optional)
1½ cups (185 g) grated uncooked red sweet potato
2 eggs
1 teaspoon ground cinnamon
1½ cups (225 g) self-raising flour, sifted
icing sugar, sifted, to dust

METHOD
Preheat the oven to 160°C. Lightly grease a 19 cm x 29 cm rectangular slice tin.

Combine the oil, sugar and dates, stand for 5 minutes. Stir in the remaining ingredients and spread the mixture into the prepared tin. Bake for about 40 minutes, then stand for 5 minutes before turning out onto a wire rack to cool. Sprinkle lightly with icing sugar and cut into slices.

Anne Smith, Mungindi, NSW

PIXIE'S DELIGHT

Makes about 24

This was one of the first recipes I copied into my first recipe book as a child, hence the basic instructions. My mum, now in her eighties, used to make this often when we were kids as we loved it. I think we really enjoyed watching the ingredients transform into marshmallow in Mum's old Sunbeam Mixmaster too.

The recipe was handwritten in Mum's recipe book along with all her other favourites; she rarely used a commercially printed cookbook. As Mum now has Alzheimer's, I can't find out the true origins of this recipe.

INGREDIENTS

125 g butter
1 cup (150 g) self-raising flour, sifted
1 cup (200 g) brown sugar
¾ cup (65 g) desiccated coconut
3 crumbled breakfast biscuits
1 teaspoon vanilla essence

Marshmallow topping
1 tablespoon powdered gelatine
½ cup (125 ml) boiling water
1 cup (220 g) sugar
desiccated coconut, to sprinkle

METHOD

Preheat the oven to 180°C. Line an 18 cm x 28 cm (approx.) slice tin with baking paper.

Melt the butter and add the other ingredients, mix. Press into the prepared tin and cook for 15 minutes. Set aside until completely cold.

To make the marshmallow topping, dissolve the gelatine in the water. Put the sugar into a bowl and pour over gelatine. Stir until dissolved. Stand a while, then whisk until thick and foamy. Spread onto the biscuit base and sprinkle with coconut. Leave to set for about 20 minutes, then cut into squares.

Note: You can colour the marshmallow with pink food colouring if you like.

Linda Yeo, Mudgee, NSW

APPLE SLICE
Makes about 15 squares

Nanna's House by Jane Larsen (aged 13 years in 1993)

When I enter smells of tea cooking,
Puddings and slices waft past my nose.
I feel warm, protected and safe.
I hear pots and pans being shuffled around,
The fire roaring, birds chirping,
And the icy wind outside.
I see Nanna standing,
Smiling and welcoming me.

I wrote this poem for Nanna who constantly cooked for the school canteen, the CWA or her grandchildren. Her Apple Slice was the greatest thing she cooked, and students and teachers alike fought for a piece at the canteen.

INGREDIENTS

8 Granny Smith apples, peeled, cored and diced
1 cup (150 g) self-raising flour
½ cup (60 g) cornflour
2 tablespoons sugar
2 tablespoons butter
½ cup (125 ml) water
1 egg yolk
cornflour, extra, to sprinkle
melted butter, sugar and ground cinnamon

METHOD

Preheat the oven to 180°C. Line the base of an 18 cm x 28 cm (approx.) slice tin with baking paper.

Cook the apples with a little water until soft, then drain well and set aside to cool. Sift the self-raising flour, cornflour and sugar into a large bowl. Rub in the butter, then mix to a stiff dough with the combined water and egg yolk.

Divide the dough in half, and roll out thinly on a floured surface. Line the prepared tin with half the pastry. Sprinkle base with a little cornflour (to prevent it going soggy), and spread with the apple. Sprinkle with a little more cornflour and cover with the rest of the pastry.

Bake for 20 minutes. Remove from the oven, brush the top with the melted butter and sprinkle with combined sugar and cinnamon.

Jane Larsen, Kojonup, WA

MACADAMIA SLICE
Makes about 16 squares

This recipe is an old American Gourmet recipe from the early 1980s. Since then I have adopted it as my own and it is my most asked-for recipe.

The slice has been to countless picnics, family functions, afternoon teas etc., and it travels well. We have even taken it to Melbourne where it joined a loaded table of lovingly-cooked goodies at a cousin's wake. Recently it made an appearance at Macca's Outside Broadcast on Australia Day in Hyde Park!

INGREDIENTS

Crust

1½ cups (225 g) plain flour, sifted
½ cup (100 g) dark brown sugar
125 g salt reduced or unsalted butter, chilled and chopped

Topping

2 eggs
1½ cups (300 g) dark brown sugar
1 teaspoon vanilla essence
½ cup (75 g) self-raising flour, sifted
1½ cups (90 g) shredded coconut
200 g finely chopped unsalted macadamia nuts
2 teaspoons fresh lemon juice
icing sugar, for decoration

METHOD

Preheat the oven to 180°C. Grease and line a 20 cm square cake tin.

Firstly, make the crust by placing the flour, sugar and butter into a food processor and processing briefly until it resembles breadcrumbs. Press the mixture into the prepared tin. Bake in the middle of the oven for 10–15 minutes or until you see that it is a pale golden colour.

To make the topping, beat the eggs with the sugar in a bowl until the mixture is thick and pale, and then stir in the vanilla essence. Gradually fold the flour into the egg mixture, then lightly fold in the coconut, macadamias and lemon juice. Smooth the topping onto the crust and bake for about 25–30 minutes or until golden.

Cool the slice in the tin, and then cut into squares and sprinkle sifted icing sugar over generously.

Jenny Heesh, Gymea Bay, NSW

MISTAKE SLICE
Makes about 18

It was Friday. Visitors were arriving Saturday, and there would be 7 children. Mother decided to bake a UN Slice. She made the slice mixture and placed it in the oven. Five minutes later, it wasn't 'doing' what it should! Mother went through the ingredients, and, oh dear, missed the flour! The mixture was yummy — now what? Mother made her pastry; turned the mistake slice onto the pastry and back into the oven. Later she topped it with chocolate. None left for Sunday!

INGREDIENTS

Nanna's special pastry
125 g butter
¼ cup (55 g) raw sugar
1 cup (150 g) self-raising flour
¾ cup (115 g) plain flour
¼ cup (30 g) cornflour
3–4 tablespoons water

Topping
125 g butter
2 tablespoon golden syrup
2 tablespoons water
1½ teaspoons bicarbonate of soda
¾ cup (65 g) dessicated coconut
¾ cup (165 g) sugar
¾ cup (35 g) crushed breakfast biscuits (about 2)

METHOD

Preheat the oven to 175°C. Grease a 28 cm x 18 cm slice tin.

To make the pastry, rub the shortening into the dry ingredients until it resembles cake crumbs. Mix together with the water. Roll out half of the dough to fit the tin (freeze the rest for another use).

To make the topping, place the shortening, golden syrup and water into a bowl and microwave for 1 minute or melt in a saucepan. Mix in the bicarb, then the coconut, sugar and breakfast biscuits. Spread on top of the pastry, and bake for 20 to 25 minutes, until golden.

Miss Margaret Corfield, Brooweena, QLD

RASPBERRY CRUMBLE SLICE

Makes about 24 squares

Everyone knows that the best raspberries in the world are grown in Scotland and Tasmania, so I chose this favourite recipe as a reminder of my early years in the UK and my husband's home in the Huon Valley, Tasmania. The fruit complements the sweet crisp crumble and base, and the semolina soaks up any juice from the raspberries, allowing the base to remain firm. It is simply delicious.

INGREDIENTS

Base

1¼ cups (185g) plain flour, sifted
1½ tablespoons raw caster sugar
125 g unsalted butter, diced
pinch of salt
1 egg, lightly beaten

Topping

⅓ cup (50 g) plain flour, sifted
¼ cup (55 g) raw caster sugar
70 g unsalted butter, diced
½ teaspoon ground cinnamon
finely grated rind of 1 lemon
½ cup (50 g) coarse porridge oats
1 tablespoon semolina
300g fresh or thawed frozen raspberries

METHOD

Preheat the oven to 200°C. Grease a 23 cm x 33 cm Swiss roll tin.

To make the base, put the flour, sugar and butter into a food processor with a pinch of salt and blitz briefly until the mixture resembles breadcrumbs. Slowly add the egg through the feeder tube and process very briefly, until just combined. Press the dough into the prepared tin and level it out with your fingers or the back of a large spoon.

To make the topping, pulse the flour, sugar, butter, cinnamon and lemon rind in a processor until just crumbly (or mix by hand). Mix in the oats with a fork so as not to break them up.

Scatter the semolina over the base in the tin, top with an even layer of raspberries and top that with the crumble mix. Press down very gently, trying to cover most of the raspberries (this may look a bit sparse, but that's okay).

Bake for 20 minutes, then turn the oven down to 180°C and bake for about 30 minutes more, until the top is golden brown. Leave to cool for about 30 minutes, then cut into squares and put on a wire rack until completely cold. Store in an airtight container for up to two days.

Lorraine Voss, Campbelltown, NSW

RHUBARB MUFFINS
Makes 12

I grew up in a family that always had a rhubarb plant in the garden, and a mother and a grandmother who had many ways to prepare it. This recipe was developed after a trip to the USA 30 years ago, where I learnt the difference between English muffins and American muffins. The rhubarb happened when we couldn't get blueberries, and I added the spices and the sugar topping to zip it up a bit. We now prefer the rhubarb to any other fruit in our muffins!

INGREDIENTS
½ cup (100 g) brown sugar
60 g butter, melted
1 egg
1 teaspoon vanilla essence
½ cup (125 ml) buttermilk
1 cup (125 g) diced rhubarb
⅓ cup (40 g) chopped walnuts
1½ cups (225 g) plain flour
½ teaspoon baking powder
½ teaspoon bicarbonate of soda
pinch salt
1 teaspoon ground cinnamon
½ teaspoon ground cloves

Topping
20 g butter, melted
2 tablespoons raw sugar
1 teaspoon ground cinnamon

Method

Preheat the oven to 220°C. Grease a 12-muffin tin.

Beat the brown sugar, butter, egg, vanilla and buttermilk together in a large mixing bowl. Stir in the rhubarb and nuts.

Sift together the flour, baking powder, bicarb, salt and spices, and fold into the wet mixture. Stir until just combined. Spoon into the prepared muffin tins.

To make the topping, combine the ingredients and sprinkle onto the muffin mixture. Bake for about 20 minutes, until firm to a gentle touch.

Susan Cole, North Perth, WA

NANA CLARKE'S CHOCOLATE SPONGE

Makes 1 or 2 filled sponges

This recipe is in memory of my Nana, Dorrie Clarke. Memories of Nana and her cooking skills go back to when I was a little girl, when I spent many happy hours with her in the kitchen.

I vividly remember going to her house on Rainbow Show day, which is still held in October. Nana would enter in all the cookery sections and we would load up suitcases of food to take to the show to be exhibited. Her sponge cakes, cream puffs and other home-baked goods always received prizes. She loved to try new recipes and was always collecting them. Nana has passed this passion on to me and I fondly remember her each time I cook.

INGREDIENTS

4 eggs, separated
½ cup (110 g) sugar
1 teaspoon bicarbonate of soda
1 dessertspoon golden syrup
½ cup (60 g) cornflour
2 dessertspoons plain flour
2 dessertspoons cocoa powder
whipped cream and chocolate icing, to decorate

METHOD

Preheat the oven to 180°C. Grease two shallow 20 cm round tins and line with baking paper.

Beat the egg whites then beat in the sugar and bicarb. Add the yolks, beat together, then add the golden syrup, and beat to combine.

Sift the flours and cocoa powder and fold into the egg mixture. Pour into the prepared tins, and bake for 20 minutes. Turn out and cool on a wire rack.

When cold, spread one cake with whipped cream and the other with chocolate icing. Place the iced cake on top of the cream. Alternatively, split the two cakes in half, fill with cream and ice both tops.

Leonie Clarke, Rainbow, VIC

NEVER-FAIL SPONGE CAKE
Makes 1 double 20 cm sponge cake

Make sure the eggs are taken from fridge a few hours before you use them, as this gives better volume when you beat them.

INGREDIENTS
4 eggs
¾ cup (165 g) sugar
¾ cup (95 g) cornflour
1 teaspoon cream of tartar
½ teaspoon bicarbonate of soda
1 teaspoon plain flour
pinch salt
whipped cream and fresh fruit, to serve

METHOD
Preheat the oven to 180°C. Grease two shallow 20 cm round tins.

Beat the eggs and sugar with electric beaters for 10–12 minutes, until very light and creamy. Sift the dry ingredients over and stir in with a knife.

Pour into the tins and bake for 10 to 15 minutes or until springy to a gentle touch.

Turn out onto a wire rack to cool. Decorate with whipped cream, passionfruit and strawberries or raspberries.

Mrs S Hudson, Summer Hill, TAS

HOME-MADE APPLE CAKES
Makes 18

My Great Aunty Glad Cooper was a great cook. She was the only girl of 8 children and never married, but she enjoyed the company of her nieces and nephews along with their families. She stayed in the family home, called The Pines, until her death in 1984 aged 78. Even though she suffered polio as a child she could cook up a storm. I was lucky to spend time with her when I was growing up, and I have memories of calling in to see her. She would be in the kitchen, or sitting waiting for family and friends in her lounge room, always with her full apron on.

I love making theses little apple cakes as it brings back many happy memories, and since her passing I have made them prize winning cakes, by entering them in the Sale Show and receiving first prize. It just shows that home-made is the best.

INGREDIENTS
- 125 g butter
- ¾ cup (165 g) caster sugar
- 2 eggs
- 2–2½ cups (300–375 g) self-raising flour, sifted
- 3 large Granny Smith apples, stewed

METHOD
Preheat the oven to 180°C. Grease 18 patty tins.

Cream the butter and sugar well. Add the eggs and beat until creamy, then slowly add the flour. You may need to add a little extra flour depending on the mixture. Roll out the dough on a floured surface to 5 mm thick. Cut rounds from the dough and use half to line the patty pans. Place a spoonful of stewed apples onto the pastry, then top with remaining pastry rounds.

Cook for about 25 minutes, until golden brown.

Note: These cakes may be iced if wished.

Karen Anderson, Clydebank, VIC

My mum's apple teacake
Makes one 20 cm round cake

This recipe was a favourite of my mother, who was a wonderful country cook. She could whip up a meal with the minimum of fuss and always find a substitute for any missing ingredient. Mum died last year and I use this recipe regularly.

INGREDIENTS
60 g butter
⅓ cup (75 g) sugar
1 egg, beaten
1 cup (150 g) self-raising flour, sifted
¼ cup (60 ml) milk
2 Granny Smith apples
1 lemon
1 teaspoon caster sugar
1 teaspoon ground cinnamon

METHOD
Preheat the oven to 180°C. Line a 20 cm round cake tin with baking paper.

Beat the butter and sugar until creamy, then beat in the egg, flour and milk.

Spoon into the prepared tin and smooth the top.

Peel the apples and cut into even wedges. Place decoratively over the top of the cake mixture. Squeeze lemon juice over the apples and sprinkle with the combined sugar and cinnamon.

Cook for 35 minutes.

Di Bayne, Mathoura, NSW

CHOCOLATE BANANA CAKE

Makes one 20 cm cake

This recipe has an unknown provenance. It's one of those recipes written down in the dim, distant past which has been in constant use ever since. It always works and is a nice twist on a plain chocolate cake.

INGREDIENTS

125 g butter
1 cup (220 g) sugar
1 tablespoon golden syrup
2 eggs
2 very ripe bananas, mashed
2 cups (300 g) plain flour, sifted
1 teaspoon baking powder, sifted
1 tablespoon cocoa powder, sifted
2 teaspoons bicarbonate of soda
220 ml milk

METHOD

Preheat the oven to 180°C. Grease a deep 20 cm round cake tin and line the base with baking paper.

Using electric beaters, cream the butter and sugar. Add the golden syrup and beat again. Add the eggs one at a time, beating until fluffy.

Stir in the bananas. Add the flour, baking powder and cocoa together and fold into the mixture. Dissolve the bicarb in the milk and stir into the mixture.

Bake for 50–60 minutes. Cake will spring back to the touch when it is cooked.

Barbara Mullaney, Melba, ACT

CHERRY CAKE

Makes one 23 cm cake

I learned to cook from my mother and since I was a teenager I always liked to be in the kitchen with her, learning her skills and her ways of preparing dishes.

Her favourite saying to me was, 'Always cook with love in your heart and whatever dish you prepare will turn out exactly right.'

Later on, after she passed away, my friends felt that 'I was born to be in the kitchen.' It is here that I put a lot of love into all my dishes that I cook, even when preparing a simple omelette.

I dedicate this recipe to my dear late mother.

INGREDIENTS

700 g natural sun-dried sultanas
1 cup (250 ml) brandy
400 g red glacé cherries
250 g butter
1½ cups (300 g) brown sugar
5 eggs
2 cups (300 g) plain flour, sifted
extra plain flour
sliced almonds

METHOD

Place the sultanas into a bowl with half the brandy, and soak overnight.

Preheat the oven to 165°C. Grease a 23 cm round cake tin and line the base and sides with buttered paper. Please see that the paper is about 6 cm above the tin like a collar.

Place the cherries into a colander to drain off the excess syrup. Slice the cherries in half (this helps the cherries not to sink to the bottom of the cake).

Using electric beaters, cream the butter and sugar together until light and fluffy. Whisk the eggs until pale and frothy and gradually beat into the butter and sugar mixture.

Fold in the flour. The mixture should be a soft dropping consistency — if it is too stiff, add a little milk. Dust the cherries with a little extra flour and place into a bowl with the sultanas. Pour the batter over the top and mix together until well combined. Pour into the prepared tin, smooth the surface and sprinkle the almonds on top.

Bake for 2½ to 3 hours, until cooked when tested with a skewer. Spoon the remaining brandy over the warm cake, and place onto a rack. Leave in the tin to cool.

Frances Miltenov, Malvern, VIC

LUCHI CAKE
Makes one 23 cm ring cake

This recipe was given to me by my darling daughter-in-law's Mum, Maria. These days it is difficult to get the family to eat any other cake, this has become such a favourite!

I thought it would be wonderful if Maria could gain some recognition outside her family for her beautiful cooking. She is Italian and the recipe came with her from Italy, though the name of the cake has been lost through time. We simply call it Luchi Cake, though perhaps it should be called Maria Luchi's Cake!

INGREDIENTS

4 medium eggs
300 g sugar
finely grated rind of 2 lemons
1 cup (250 ml) olive oil
310 g self-raising flour
1 teaspoon vanilla essence
30 ml rum
pinch of salt
small squeeze lemon juice
200–250 g cooking chocolate (more is better!)
1 teaspoon of cocoa powder mixed with a few good drops of milk

METHOD

Preheat the oven to 175°C. Grease a 23 cm, 8-cup capacity fluted ring tin.

In a mixer, beat the eggs, sugar and lemon rind on high speed until thick and creamy. Reduce the speed and gradually add the oil. Beat until well combined. Add the flour slowly and fold in by hand.

Add the vanilla essence, rum, salt and lemon juice.

Melt the chocolate, cocoa and milk in a bowl over a pan of simmering water. Add some of the cake mixture to the melted chocolate and mix in.

Pour some cake mixture into the prepared tin, then a layer of the chocolate mixture. Alternate the two until finished. Bake for 35–45 minutes, testing every 5 minutes after 35 mins. Cool in the tin before turning out.

Note: You can use half oil and half butter if you like, though the olive oil makes a really moist cake.

Kali Hammond, Lindfield, NSW

SIMPLICITY CHOCOLATE CAKE

Makes one 20 cm x 30 cm cake

My 4-year-old grandson helps me make this chocolate cake almost every week and proceeds to eat it while still hot with no icing. I've made this cake for over 40 years from New Australian Cookery Illustrated *and it never fails. It's the only chocolate cake my family will eat.*

INGREDIENTS

60 g softened butter
2 tablespoons cocoa powder, sifted
1 cup (150 g) self-raising flour, sifted
1 cup (220 g) sugar
½ cup (125 ml) milk
2 eggs
½ teaspoon vanilla or almond essence

METHOD

Preheat the oven to 170°C. Grease a 20 cm x 30 cm lamington tin.

Place all the ingredients into a bowl and, using electric beaters, beat for 3 minutes on high speed. Transfer to the prepared tin and bake for 20 minutes, until cooked when tested with a skewer. Cool, then ice with chocolate icing.

Do not overcook this cake, it should be very moist.

Dorothy Pickering, Gunnedah, NSW

DORMCAKE
Makes about 1 cake

'Dormcake' was invented by my youngest daughter when she was four years old. It seems she held no adult inhibition on the combination of flavours and textures. And we loved the end result!

The name 'dorm' is short for dormouse (don't let it put you off your cake!), which is one of Bridgette's nicknames. Where the nickname came from is already one of those family mysteries. The most likely origin (by family consensus), was some time on our trip around Oz back in 2001.

INGREDIENTS
1 cup (150 g) self-raising flour
¼ to ½ cup (55 g–110 g) caster sugar
cocoa (desired amount)
water
nutmeg (big sprinkle)
2 eggs
weeties (small sprinkle)

METHOD
Preheat the oven to 170°C.

Mix all the ingredients together and place into a heart-shaped tin. Bake for about 30 minutes.

Bridgette Carman, Dongara, WA

Rich Christmas cake
Makes one 20 cm cake

My rich fruit Christmas cakes have become popular over 28 years of baking them. I have increased the fruit content, and include lots of almonds in the recipe as well as on the top of the cakes. It is the moist richness which seems to attract customers.

In October each year, we begin a big bake-up to raise money for Bush Church Aid (BCA). Last Christmas we, all volunteers, raised over $8500 and in doing so, cooked 1127 cakes. Believe it or not, I ended up without a cake for myself!

Ingredients

180 g butter
1 cup (200 g) light brown sugar
1½ teaspoons mixed spice
1½ teaspoons bicarbonate of soda
1 cup (250 ml) water
500 g mixed fruit
250 g raisins
250 g sultanas
180 g whole red glacé cherries
125 g mixed peel
180 g almonds
2 tablespoons plum or apricot jam
2 tablespoons orange or pineapple juice
1 dessertspoon Parisian essence
2 eggs, well beaten
1 cup (150 g) self-raising flour, sifted
1 cup (150 g) plain flour, sifted
extra almonds, to decorate

METHOD

Preheat the oven to 200°C. Grease a 20 cm round cake tin and line with baking paper.

Combine the butter, sugar, spice, bicarb, water, all the fruit, almonds, jam, juice and Parisian essence in a large saucepan. Bring to the boil, then reduce the heat slightly and simmer for 10 minutes.

Cool slightly, then add the eggs and flours. Stir to combine.

Transfer to the prepared tin, and decorate with extra almonds. Place cake into the oven, and reduce the heat to 150°C after a few minutes. Cook for one hour until skewer comes out cleanly.

Margaret Kidney OAM, Magill, SA

FARMER'S CAKES
Makes about 34

This recipe has been in the Kennedy family for over 100 years. Sophie Kennedy (83 years old) would bake at least a batch of cakes each week.

INGREDIENTS

6 cups (900 g) plain flour, sifted
1 tablespoon ground nutmeg
2 cups (440 g) sugar
5 teaspoons baking powder
125 g butter
2½ cups (435 g) sultanas, or mixed dried fruit
3 eggs, lightly beaten
about 1½ cups (375 ml) milk

METHOD

Preheat the oven to 210°C. Lightly grease 2 baking trays.

Place all the dry ingredients into a big bowl. Using your fingertips, rub in the butter. Then mix in the fruit.

Whisk the eggs and milk together. Add to the dry ingredients and mix together. If too dry, add a little more milk to make the consistency of a scone dough.

Press out by hand on a floured surface to 3 cm thick. Cut out with 5 cm scone cutter. Bake for 15 minutes, until golden.

Sophie Kennedy, Fernmount, NSW

KILKENNY BOILED FRUITCAKE
Makes one 20 cm round cake

This recipe comes from my Uncle Miff who has always been a bit of a 'bush cook', and now makes the most wonderful boiled fruit cake you have ever tasted. The secret ingredient is butterscotch cream liqueur. Rather than have him give me a cake every time I visit him, I finally pleaded for the recipe and the secret ingredient. He relented and now I also pass on this exciting morsel of food to other family and friends.

INGREDIENTS
375g mixed fruit
1 cup (220 g) sugar
1 teaspoon mixed spice
1 cup (250 ml) water
125g butter
½ cup (125 ml) butterscotch liqueur
2 eggs, lightly beaten
2 cups (300 g) self-raising flour, sifted
1 teaspoon bicarbonate of soda
pinch salt

METHOD
Preheat the oven to 170°C. Grease and line a 20 cm round cake tin.

Place the fruit, sugar, spice, water and butter into a large saucepan and bring to the boil. Reduce the heat and simmer gently for about 5 minutes, then remove from the heat and allow to cool.

Add the liqueur and eggs, mix well. Fold in the flour, bicarb and salt and mix well. Place mixture into the prepared tin, and bake for 1–1¼ hours or until cooked when tested with a skewer.

Note: I have sometimes added 2 tablespoons of pineapple jam or marmalade, this goes in with the eggs. Irish cream liqueur can be substituted for the butterscotch cream liqueur if you like.

Jacky Lynch, Coorparoo, QLD

Aunty E's fruit cake
Makes one 25 cm round cake

My Aunty Elaine is an amazing lady. She has worked tirelessly for years in the family business, doing the books and the pays. With three children and their respective children, Elaine always found time to help with looking after grandkids, helping with moving, cleaning, washing etc. Amazingly, after all this, she still found time to keep her own house immaculate and be an amazing cook.

I will always remember Elaine for her Christmas cake. Being a chef myself, I have tasted many wonderful and varied foods, but I just can't go past Elaine's cake. When Elaine would holiday at her caravan on the Central Coast I used to love to go and visit her. I initially told her I went to see her and Uncle John, but she soon figured out the real reason was because I knew she would have some cake left. We had a talk about the cake one day and she seemed a little reluctant to part with the recipe. I told her she wasn't allowed to take this recipe to the grave. I must have pressed the right buttons, for a few weeks later this recipe arrived on the fax.

Ingredients

750 g sultanas
500 g seeded raisins
500 g currants
500 g mixed dried fruit
250 g mixed peel
125 g glacé pineapple, chopped
125 g glacé apricots, quartered
250 g glacé cherries
1 cup (250 ml) water
1 cup (250 ml) rum or brandy
500 g butter
375 g brown sugar

250 g caster sugar
finely grated rind of 1 orange
finely grated rind of 1 lemon
1 tablespoon treacle or golden syrup
1 teaspoon bicarbonate of soda
10 eggs, lightly beaten
500 g plain flour, sifted
125 g self-raising flour, sifted
¼ teaspoon salt
1 tablespoon Parisian essence, optional
extra rum or brandy

METHOD

Put the fruit into a large saucepan. Add the water, rum, butter and sugars. Bring gently to the boil, stirring occasionally, then remove from the heat. Add the citrus rind, treacle and bicarb, mix in thoroughly. Transfer to a large bowl, cover and leave to stand overnight.

Preheat the oven to 150°C. Line a 25 cm cake tin with 2 layers of foil or baking paper.

Pour the eggs onto the fruit mixture, add the flours and salt, and mix thoroughly. Add enough Parisian essence to give the cake the desired colour, if you like. Spread the mixture evenly into the prepared cake tin. Bake for 5–5½ hours, until cooked when tested with a skewer. Remove from oven and sprinkle with a good slurp of rum or brandy. When cold, cover with greaseproof paper and a few thicknesses of newspaper.

Note: I leave the fruit soaking for several days after boiling up. I don't use Parisian essence. The cake can be cooked in two smaller tins for 3–3½ hours.

Gavin Ashby, Coleambally, NSW

DUTCH GINGER CAKE

Makes one 20 cm round cake

My mother-in-law made this every Christmas for me until she died a few years ago. Both of us loved ginger. The first time she made it for me was for the gathering of the family after the funeral of my little cot-death baby, Edward, so forever this cake is linked to my mother-in-law, Kath Pearce.

INGREDIENTS

1¾ cups (265 g) plain flour, sifted
pinch salt
1 cup (220 g) caster sugar
4 oz (125 g) glacé ginger, finely chopped
6 oz butter, melted and cooled
1 egg, lightly beaten
slivered or whole blanched almonds, to decorate

METHOD

Preheat the oven to 180°C. Grease a 20 cm round cake tin and line with baking paper.

Mix together the flour, salt and caster sugar in a bowl. Add the glacé ginger and cooled butter. Add most of the beaten egg (reserve some of the beaten egg to glaze the cake). Spread the mixture into the prepared tin, and decorate the top with almonds. Brush with the reserved beaten egg.

Bake for 45 minutes to 1 hour until it is golden brown. Cool completely in the tin.

Carolyn Pearce, Cherrybrook, NSW

MIRIAM'S HAZELNUT CAKE

Makes one 20 cm round cake

This cake was made by my mother-in-law Miriam Gerstel. She was a fantastic cook who enjoyed cooking rich and tasty food for her family and friends. She always used good ingredients.

This hazelnut cake was her specialty. The secret is to grind the nuts yourself so that you get that rich hazelnut flavour.

Unfortunately she passed away a few years ago, but we remember her wicked sense humour and her kindness.

INGREDIENTS

5 x 60 g eggs, separated
180 g caster sugar
250 g roasted hazelnuts, skinned and ground

Chocolate cream
250 ml pouring cream
120 g dark chocolate, chopped

METHOD

Preheat the oven to 180°C. Grease and line a 20 cm round cake tin.

Beat the egg yolks with the sugar until thick and pale. Fold in the hazelnuts. Beat the egg whites until they form firm peaks and then fold into hazelnut mixture. Pour into the prepared tin.

Bake for 50–55 minutes or until a skewer comes out clean. Turn out onto a wire rack to cool completely.

To make the chocolate cream, whip the cream until thick. Melt the chocolate in a heat proof bowl over simmering water. Pour the chocolate into the cream and combine.

Use a serrated knife to slice the cake in half horizontally. Cover the bottom half with some of the chocolate cream, place top of cake over cream and then spread remaining cream over sides and top of cake.

Diane Temple, Castlecrag, NSW

PUMPKIN TEA BAG CAKE

Makes one 22 cm round cake

The Pumpkin Tea Bag Cake recipe was discovered when an Aussie tea bag brand was re-launched many years ago. The original recipe was in pre-metric, imperial measurements. I first heard it on ABC Radio on a weekend program with Bob Hughes. A week after the re-launch, Bob made the recipe and presented it on air.

INGREDIENTS

1 cup (250 ml) boiling water
4 tea bags
125g butter
1 cup (220 g) caster sugar
1 tablespoon golden syrup
500g mixed dried fruit (any combination)
1 cup (260 g) cold mashed pumpkin (press out excess moisture)
2 eggs, lightly beaten
1 cup (150 g) plain flour, sifted
1 cup (150 g) self-raising flour, sifted
1 teaspoon ground cinnamon
1 teaspoon bicarbonate of soda

METHOD

Preheat the oven to 180°C. Line a 22 cm round cake tin with baking paper.

Pour the boiling water onto the tea bags. Stand until almost cold, then squeeze the bags to extract all flavours. Discard the bags.

Put the brewed tea into a saucepan with the butter, sugar, golden syrup and fruit and bring to the boil. Reduce the heat and simmer very gently for 5–10 minutes. Remove from the heat and leave to cool.

Add the pumpkin and eggs, mix in well then stir in the flours, cinnamon and bicarb.

Pour into the prepared tin and bake for 30 minutes, then reduce the heat to 160°C. Cook for a further 1–1½ hours, until cooked when tested with a skewer. Cool in the tin, then turn out. The cake will keep for a week in an air tight container.

Note: If you like, you can add 2 tablespoons of Grand Marnier or whisky (add to mixture after stirring through flours and spice), or spoon it over the cake after baking and while still hot. Don't pour spirits directly into the centre of the cake as this can cause the cake to fall.

Noeline Walk, Fraser Island, QLD

Rum syrup cake

Makes one 23 cm baba cake

I created this cake when we were looking for a recipe to tie in with the theme for the Nambour Sugar Festival a few years ago.

Ingredients

½ cup (70 g) finely chopped pecans
250 g butter
1 cup (220 g) caster sugar
½ teaspoon vanilla essence
3 eggs, separated
⅓ cup (80 ml) dark rum
⅔ cup (170 ml) buttermilk
2 cups (300 g) self-raising flour, sifted

Syrup
1 cup (220 g) sugar
½ cup (125 ml) water
½ cup (125 ml) dark rum

METHOD

Preheat the oven to 180°C. Grease a 23 cm, 8-cup capacity baba tin very well with butter. Sprinkle the pecans into the tin, rolling to coat the sides.

Using electric beaters, beat the butter, sugar and vanilla essence until creamy, then beat in the egg yolks, one at a time. Combine the rum and buttermilk, and add in two batches, alternating with the flour.

Beat the egg whites in a small bowl until soft peaks form. Fold gently into the cake mixture. Spoon into the prepared tin and bake for 40–50 minutes, until cooked when tested with a skewer. Just before the cake is ready, make the syrup.

To make the syrup, combine the sugar, water and rum in a saucepan. Stir over medium heat until the sugar dissolves, then bring to a rolling boil. Boil for 4 minutes, stirring constantly.

Take the cake from the oven and while still hot, prick the cake all over with a skewer. Drizzle with the hot syrup. Allow the syrup to absorb into the cake, and cool before turning onto a serving plate.

Serve in slices with whipped cream and fresh fruit as desired.

Sonia Benesovsky, Nambour, QLD

Princes cake (Fyrstekake)

Serves 8–10

Mashed Potato? In a cake? You must be joking!

That's the reaction we always get when we serve this sinfully rich and utterly delicious almond-filled cake for the first time. My grandmother brought the recipe with her from Norway to New Zealand in 1939, and for a long time she was reluctant to give it to anyone outside the family — and who can blame her. It was her little secret, and she was famous for it. She is gone now, but in the family her memory lives on every time we serve her special cake.

INGREDIENTS

Shortcrust pastry

150 g butter
125 g sugar
2 tablespoons cream
1 egg yolk
1⅔ cup (250 g) plain flour, sifted
1 tablespoon baking powder

Filling

150 g ground almonds
1 cup (220 g) sugar
60 g butter, melted
2 egg yolks
½ teaspoon ground cinnamon
1 teaspoon almond essence
½ cup (150 g) mashed potato
2 egg whites

METHOD

Preheat the oven to 180°C. Grease a 25 cm springform tin.

To make the shortcrust pastry, cream the butter and sugar, then beat in the cream and egg yolk. Stir in the flour and baking powder. Press ⅔ of the mixture into the base of the prepared tin. Reserve the rest for the top.

To make the filling, mix the almonds, sugar, melted butter, egg yolks, cinnamon, almond essence and mashed potato. Beat the egg whites until firm peaks form, and fold into the potato mixture.

Pour into the pastry shell. Roll out the reserved dough, and cut into strips. Decorate the top with the strips arranged in a lattice pattern. Bake for about 40 minutes.

Jon Moen, Currumbin, QLD

MUM'S DROUGHT AND DEPRESSION CAKE
Makes one 20 cm cake

The name says it all, doesn't it? But this is quite a good cake, featured in many a school lunch and shearer's or stack builder's tea basket.

Nowadays, it's suitable for low-fat, low sugar or egg-free diets.

INGREDIENTS
    1 tablespoon dripping
    1 tablespoon sugar
    pinch salt
    1 cup (260 g) warm, cooked and mashed pumpkin
    1 teaspoon bicarbonate of soda
    1 cup (250 ml) reconstituted powdered milk
    2 cups (300 g) plain flour, sifted
    1½ teaspoons cream of tartar
    1 teaspoon finely grated orange rind
    1–2 teaspoons mixed spice, optional
    1 cup (150 g) currants
    1 cup (175 g) sultanas

METHOD
Preheat the oven to 180°C. Grease and line a 20 cm round cake tin.

Combine the dripping, sugar, salt and pumpkin in a bowl. Mix the bicarb with milk and add to the pumpkin mixture, then stir in flour, cream of tartar, rind and spice. Add the fruit last. Spread into the prepared tin.

Bake for 1–1½ hours, until cooked when tested with a skewer.

Note: These days you would use butter or margarine, and fresh milk. Also, you could add ½ cup (125 ml) sherry or spirits, with a little more poured over cake when removed from oven.

Mrs K Clancy, Holbrook, NSW

Scones

Makes about 10

This is a favourite recipe of my family and friends. It was given to me as a young married woman in 1957 by the helpful older lady next door. We had just moved into our new house, which was far from completed, but we thought we were kings. We had a new baby as well, so cooking was not one of my priorities! I lost contact with this lady, though strangely enough I renewed our friendship when I came across her at my Probus Club. After 40 years we have taken up where we left off!

The recipe intrigues everyone because of leaving the oven door open, but it really works and the scones are light and lovely.

INGREDIENTS

2 cups (300 g) self-raising flour, sifted
pinch salt
1 tablespoon sugar
1 cup (250 ml) milk
1 teaspoon melted butter
1 egg

METHOD

Preheat the oven to 200C.

In a bowl, mix the flour, salt and sugar. Combine the milk, butter and egg. Add to the dry ingredients and mix well.

Knead 3 times, then press out and cut into scone shapes. Place onto an oven tray, and place into the oven. Leave the door open for 5 minutes, then close the door for 7 minutes.

Glennie Hodgson, Swansea Heads, NSW

VINNIE'S BUN
Serves about 15

Here is a damper I make for my friends at Vinnie's. I take it down as soon as it is made and it is yummy! This is suitable for diabetics, and can be served plain or buttered.

INGREDIENTS
⅔ cup (120 g) pitted dates, chopped
½ cup (90 g) dried apricots
½ cup (85 g) sultanas
½ cup (125 ml) boiling water
½ teaspoon bicarbonate of soda
2 cups (300 g) plain flour, sifted
pinch salt
1 large egg
300 ml cream
a little milk

METHOD
Put the dried fruit into bowl and add boiling water and bicarb. Cover and soak overnight or until cool.

Preheat the oven to 200°C.

Add the flour and salt to the fruit. Combine the egg and cream and add to mixture. Mix with a knife to a sticky dough. If it is too dry, add a little bit of milk.

Turn onto a floured surface, and shape into a damper about 6 cm thick. Mark into segments, and brush with milk. Cook for 45 minutes, until golden brown and cooked through.

Marion Phillis, Mittagong, NSW

OMA'S HONEYBREAD
Makes lots!

This recipe for Oma's honeybread is a staple filler in our household. It is a German recipe handed down to me by my mother. Rather than eating chips and commercial biscuits, we use this recipe to make everyday biscuits, using the biggest cookie cutter shapes we have. I then make a rather runny icing, slap some on each biscuit and sprinkle with 100s and 1000s. For more festive occasions, we use special cutters such as Easter bunnies and Xmas trees, and the kids and I make many fancy decorations using small lollies.

INGREDIENTS
    1 teaspoon bicarbonate of soda
    1 tablespoon water
    1 kg plain flour, sifted
    500 g sugar
    300 g honey
    6 eggs
    1 teaspoon cinnamon
    1 teaspoon ground cloves

METHOD
Preheat the oven to 200°C. Line two baking trays with baking paper.

Dissolve the bicarb in the water. Place all the ingredients into a mixer with a dough hook attachment (the mixer must have a strong motor). Mix until combined.

Roll out the mixture, using plain flour to stop dough sticking, to about 5 mm thick. Cut out desired shapes, and arrange onto trays. Bake for 10–12 minutes.

Note: The mixture can also be frozen until ready to use. Store in an ice-cream container dusted with flour.

Irene Zeitler, Malvern, VIC

NEVER-FAIL CURRANT LOAF
Makes one loaf

My recipe is the world's easiest! I remember making this with my mum when I was tiny. My 2½-year-old daughter now helps me make it. The recipe traditionally uses currants, but successful variations have used fruit medley, sultanas, raisins and dates. Ensure youngsters are supervised with the hot tea bit, and yes, it really only has 4 ingredients — there is no shortening or eggs. It is also useful in that you can start making it, leave it and come back to it — very handy when you have young children. It is also cheap and very yummy! This loaf keeps very well and is great for lunch boxes.

INGREDIENTS
1 cup (150 g) currants
1 cup (220 g) sugar
1 cup (250 ml) hot strong tea
2 cups (300 g) self-raising flour

METHOD
Mix the currants, sugar and tea together until the sugar has dissolved. Wander off and do other things until the tea cools.

Preheat the oven to 180°C. Grease a loaf tin.

Mix the flour into the currant mixture, and pour into the prepared tin. Bake for 45 minutes, or until a skewer comes out clean. Cool on a wire rack.

Serve sliced and buttered.

Ceri Davies, Latrobe, TAS

BILLY BUSH DOG'S PUMPKIN DAMPER

Makes 1 large damper

This pumpkin damper is a little different because it is a bit sweeter than bread damper. Pumpkin damper is good to have in the afternoon or evening instead of having sweets. Like all dampers, you just wrap them up in a tea towel to keep them.

While on the wallaby, it is great to be able to just pull up and break out a chunk of pumpkin damper and have a hot mug of billy tea. What a way to go!

It makes you want to keep on travelling around just to try out recipes and test your skills in the art of camp-oven cooking.

INGREDIENTS

5 cups (750 g) self-raising flour, sifted
½ teaspoon baking powder
2 dessertspoons powdered milk
2 dessertspoons raw or brown sugar
2 pinches cooking salt
½ cup (60 g) sultanas
2 good dobs butter, at room temperature
1 cup (260 g) cooked mashed pumpkin
1 egg, beaten
water
flour, extra

METHOD

In a bowl, add the flour, baking powder, powdered milk, sugar, salt and sultanas, and mix well. Add the butter and rub in until it feels like breadcrumbs. Mix in the pumpkin and egg, adding enough water (a bit at a time) to make a soft dough. If it becomes too wet, just sprinkle a bit of flour on the damper. Remember not to over knead the damper.

Pre-warm a camp oven at the edge of the fire. Place 4 shovels of coals from the fire into a shallow hole. Flour the bottom of the camp oven. Place the damper into the oven, and cover with the lid. Place the oven onto the coals, then place 2 shovels of coals on top.

Cook for about 35 minutes, until crusty. Remove the oven from the coals and lift the damper from the oven. Place onto a rack. Cover with a tea towel and let cool.

Billy Bush Dog, Mudgee, NSW

PRESERVES

To prepare jars for jams and preserves, preheat the oven to 150°C. Wash the jars and lids in hot soapy water, and rinse well. Arrange upside down on a rack over a baking tray and place into the oven to dry them thoroughly, then turn off the heat and leave in the oven until needed, to keep warm to hot. Time this according to how long your recipe takes. Hot filling must go into hot jars. If they go into cold jars the glass may break — disaster! Seal the jars tightly with the lid, taking care while handling hot jars. When cool, label and date each jar.

Grape Jam

Makes about 8 cups (2 L)

During the year 1800, having been granted 2000 acres of land at Bathurst, NSW, the Sutor family set to work establishing their farming enterprise. In doing so, they planted Isabella Grapes, from which cuttings were taken for us. After quarantine, we planted them at Barmera, SA.

This story forms part of Australia's agricultural history, which we feel should be preserved. Isabella grapes are prized for making Grape Jam, whilst the Sutor family continues to farm on their Bathurst property. It is the oldest operating business in Australia! This recipe is courtesy of Mrs Tyrell, of the wine-making family.

INGREDIENTS

3 kg Isabella grapes
1 cup water
sugar
juice of 2 lemons

METHOD

Wash the grapes and remove the stalks. Place in a preserving pan with water. Boil gently for 10 minutes, or a little longer, until grapes are softened, juice flows and seeds float.

Skim the seeds (we put the whole load through a sieve) and add one cup of sugar to one cup of pulp. Add the lemon juice. Boil quickly until set and the mixture drops thickly from spoon when tested. Pour into jars and seal immediately.

Makes the greatest jam!

Note: If Isabella grapes are unavailable, you could use muscatels.

Yvonne and Rex Bakes, Barmirra, SA

Nana's Apple Chutney
Makes 12 cups (3 L)

This was my mother's recipe, and she got it from her mother. It is great with pork, beef and lamb, or you can use it like jam on toast. When my wife first made this recipe she left the cayenne pepper out and Mum picked it up straight away. I grew up with chutney on everything including cheese sandwiches, and I still think it is great.

Ingredients

1 kg green apples, peeled and cored
1 kg onions
1 kg raisins
5 cups (1.25 L) vinegar, approximately
1 kg sugar
500 g treacle
1 teaspoon salt
1 teaspoon cayenne pepper
4 or 5 cloves

Method

Finely chop the apples, onions and raisins. Place into a large saucepan, and add enough vinegar to cover. Bring to the boil then add the rest of ingredients, stirring to dissolve the sugar. Simmer for 1 hour, until thick. Pour into jars and seal immediately.

Barry Hicks, Won Wron, VIC

PEACH CHUTNEY
Makes 7 cups (1.75 L)

This was Ted Moloney's recipe from the Herald in the 1960s or 70s. It is absolutely the best!

INGREDIENTS
   2 kg ripe peaches, peeled and roughly diced
   250 g seedless raisins
   1 medium white onion, minced
   1 small clove garlic, crushed
   1 dessertspoon chilli powder
   1 scant dessertspoon very finely chopped fresh ginger
   1 scant dessertspoon salt
   3 cups (750 ml) white vinegar
   2¾ cups (750 g) brown sugar

METHOD
Place all of the ingredients into a preserving pan or large saucepan. Bring to the boil and keep at a simmer for 1–1½ hours, or until a thick chutney consistency.

   Season with a little salt to taste. Pour into jars and seal immediately.

Carolyn Pearce, Cherrybrook, NSW

BBQ TOMATO SAUCE
Makes 10 cups (2.5 L)

This recipe has been handed down by my dear old mum, so it has been made for many years. I have made slight changes, by using brown vinegar instead of white, and raw sugar instead of white sugar. I just find this gives more body and a richer colour.

INGREDIENTS
3 kg tomatoes, chopped
500 g onions, chopped
4 large garlic cloves, chopped
15 g cloves
15 g ground ginger
pinch cayenne pepper
⅓ cup (90 g) salt
1 kg raw sugar
2½ cups (625 ml) brown vinegar

METHOD
Combine the tomatoes, onion, garlic, spices and salt in a large saucepan. Bring to the boil. Reduce the heat and simmer for 2 hours, stirring occasionally.

Press through a sieve to separate the mixture. Place the solids into a vitamiser (blender or food processor), and blend to a purée. Return to the pan with the liquid, and add the sugar and vinegar. Stir over medium heat until the sugar has dissolved, then simmer again for 1 hour, until it is the consistency of thick cream. Pour into jars or bottles and seal immediately.

Lee McLeish, Hurstbridge, VIC

CURRIED TOMATO RELISH
Makes 10 cups (2.5 L)

The following recipe was given to me by the late Mrs Hilda Dawes (my brother's mother-in-law) in 1953, the year I was married. I have made it each year since and without a failure — not bad for a very average cook! It is particularly nice on a good barbeque steak and even on sausages. We enjoy it with roast beef also.

INGREDIENTS
    3 kg tomatoes (I prefer home grown as they have more flavour)
    1 kg brown onions
    ½ cup (140 g) salt
    1 kg sugar
    3 tablespoons curry powder
    3 tablespoons mustard powder
    ¼ cup (60 ml) white vinegar
    freshly ground pepper

METHOD
Cut the tomatoes and onions into small bite-sized pieces. Sprinkle both well with salt and stand overnight. Strain through a colander.

Place the tomatoes, onions and sugar into a large saucepan, stirring to dissolve the sugar. Bring to the boil and cook for 5 minutes. Mix the curry powder, mustard powder and pepper with the vinegar, and add to the saucepan. Return to the boil, reduce the heat and simmer for 1 hour, stirring occasionally. Pour into jars and seal immediately.

This will keep for at least year.

Margaret Norton, Armidale, NSW

Green Tomato and Cucumber Pickles

Makes 28 cups (7 L)

I first had these pickles at my in-laws' home in the Riverland, where the seasonal glut of home-grown fruit and vegetables was preserved for use during the year. At their home for lunch there was always some type of cold meat, usually pickled pork or corned beef, fresh tomatoes and apple cucumbers (as many as you could eat!), fresh bread and pickles.

My mother-in-law was a very resilient lady. In the 1940s, she left her first husband in Adelaide and travelled to the Riverland with her 2 young boys to housekeep for my father-in-law, a widower with 6 young children. They later married and produced another 5 children and so there were always many mouths to feed. She could make a little go a long way, no one was ever hungry and all her cooking was done on a wood-fired stove. She didn't even have the luxury of a slow combustion stove — just a little green Metters No. 2. These pickles are dedicated to Elsie.

Ingredients

500 g salt

16 cups (4 L) water

2 kg green tomatoes, chopped

2 kg cucumbers, unpeeled and sliced

2 kg onions, cut into thin wedges

5 cups (1.1 kg) sugar

2 cups (300 g) plain flour, sifted

1½ tablespoons ground turmeric

2 teaspoons white pepper

2 tablespoons curry powder

2 tablespoons mustard powder

9 cups (2.25 L) vinegar

2 teaspoons ground allspice

METHOD

Dissolve the salt in the water. Place the tomatoes, cucumbers and onions into a large saucepan (not aluminium). Pour the salted water over and let stand overnight. Place over high heat, bring to the boil and cook for 5 minutes. Remove from the heat and drain well.

Combine the sugar, flour, turmeric, pepper, curry powder and mustard powder, and mix to a paste with 3 cups (750 ml) cold water.

Place the vinegar and allspice into a large saucepan and bring to the boil. Stir in the paste mixture and return to the boil. Add the vegetables, stir to combine. Pour into jars and seal immediately.

Note: Recipe may be halved if you like.

Mrs Kathy Pfeiffer, Athelstone, SA

Robyn's Vegetable Pickles
Makes 10 cups (2.5 L)

Many years ago, Robyn and I would be together on 'fire spotting duty' at the top of the Berowra Fire Tower. In between looking out for signs of fire, recording wind velocity etc, we would be swapping recipes. She was a brilliant cook. I say 'was', because sadly she's no longer with us. I especially love this recipe as it is both delicious and a way of perpetuating her memory.

Ingredients
3 medium zucchini
3 medium Lebanese cucumbers
3 medium onions
3 red capsicums
3 medium carrots
½ cup (140 g) salt
3¼ cups (810 ml) good white vinegar
2 cups (440 g) sugar
2 heaped teaspoons curry powder
1 teaspoon celery seeds
1 teaspoon mustard seeds

Method

Cut the vegetables into rounds, strips or bite-sized pieces. Place into a large container (not aluminium), and cover with water into which the salt has been dissolved. Stand for half a day, then drain and rinse.

In a large saucepan, combine the vinegar, sugar, curry powder and seeds. Stir over medium heat until the sugar has dissolved, then bring to the boil. Add the vegetables and return to the boil. Reduce the heat and simmer gently for two or three minutes. Pour into jars and seal immediately.

Cool to room temperature, then keep refrigerated. They last many weeks in the fridge.

Ann Jennings, Woolgoolga, NSW

PICKLED ZUCCHINI
Makes 5 cups (1.25 L)

These are nice with cheese or salami, or on small biscuits as a nibble, accompanied by wine or other drinks.

INGREDIENTS

- 1 kg small zucchini, thinly sliced
- 2 medium onions, thinly sliced
- ¼ cup (70 g) salt
- 2 cups (500 ml) white vinegar
- 2 teaspoons mustard seeds
- 1 teaspoon caraway seeds
- 2 teaspoons turmeric
- 1 cup (220 g) white sugar

METHOD

Place the zucchini and onion into a large bowl with the salt and cover with water. Leave to stand for 2 hours. I put the onion at one end so that I may easily remove it before the zucchini. If you find this difficult, then place the zucchini and onion into separate containers.

About half an hour before the 2 hours is up, place the vinegar, mustard seeds, caraway seeds, turmeric and sugar into a large saucepan. Slowly bring to the boil, stirring regularly until the sugar dissolves.

Place the onion into a colander and rinse under cold running water to remove as much of the salt as possible. Drain well. Add to the boiling vinegar mixture and cook for 7–10 minutes, until just soft but still slightly crisp. While the onions are cooking, rinse and drain the zucchini. Add the zucchini to the saucepan, return to the boil and cook for about 5 minutes. Pour into jars and seal immediately.

Note: If you have a food processor, use it to slice the vegetables as it saves a lot of time and slices thinly.

Helen Cretan, Lavington, NSW

INDEX